ıting

Soccer – Dribbling and Feinting

68 Drills and Exercises Designed to Improve Dribbling and Feinting

Thomas Dooley & Christian Titz

Meyer & Meyer Sport

Photo & Illustration Credits:

Cover Photos: © fotolia, Melinda Nagy, © fotolia, © fotolia/Rainer Claus
Cover Design: Sabine Groten
Illustrations: Easy2Coach Draw

British Library Cataloguing in Publication Data
A catalogue record for this book is available from the British Library

Thomas Dooley & Christian Titz
Soccer – Dribbling and Feinting
Maidenhead: Meyer & Meyer Sport (UK) Ltd., 2010
ISBN 978-1-84126-301-4

Aachen, Adelaide, Auckland, Budapest, Cape Town, Graz, Indianapolis, Maidenhead, Olten (CH), Singapore, Toronto
Member of the World
Sport Publishers' Association (WSPA)
www.w-s-p-a.org

Printed and bound by: B.O.S.S Druck und Medien GmbH, Germany
ISBN 978-1-84126-301-4
E-Mail: info@m-m-sports.com
www.m-m-sports.com

Table of contents

Table of contents

Foreword

As I first turned my thoughts toward writing this training material I was very quickly drawn to the fascination of this topic. Until then, I had never found all the coaching subjects covered in one book. Finally we have such a book. It is impressive how many aspects of coaching in the various chapters are covered with the help of endless exercises and drills. I believe that this book is unique throughout the world and quite simply a must for anyone interested in soccer. We are already experiencing a great deal of success with these coaching concepts.

With the help of this book, this topic is complete. In addition to the book, we offer further books with coaching exercises for differing age groups and many practical, useful tips for coaches and players alike. Personally, for me, it was important that there was something here for everybody. You will notice, when reading closely, that we always speak of the player as 'he'. This form has only been used to simplify the writing proces and does, of course, include all girl and women players. Because one thing is clear - this book is aimed at anyone interested in soccer, irrespective of gender.

The symbiosis of practice-related coaching sessions on the pitch through the graphical and text descriptions to the complete application of the drills is fascinating. This proves the point that without a structured concept, successful coaching is simply not possible.

Enjoy reading, and learning.

Sincerely,

Thomas Dooley

Description of Dribbling and Feinting

Good ball skills and the ability to master different techniques, tricks and movements at a high tempo are basic skills of modern soccer of every player.

The following book is a modern training aid which helps the player to learn the most important dribbling techniques, tricks and juggling skills. Through clear language, numerous graphics, and the introduction of countless methodological and didactic tips, this book will fast become an essential guide for both player and trainer.

The exercises presented in this book are notable for their differing levels of difficulty and variation of skills. They allow the different juggling skills, dribbling techniques, body swerves and ball tricks to be coached to differing age groups.

Fine skills and coordination are developed with these exercise examples. These important drills should be regularly trained in all junior age groups as well as in senior soccer. For older players, they serve to preserve existing skills as well as developing the technique and movement of younger players.

The book is not only a detailed collection of all important ball skills and movements, it also describes how to implement these drills and apply the right correction with extreme clarity and ease of understanding.

Criteria of Skills Training

The following is a list of criteria which should be adhered to during a skills training session. These tips are helpful for coach and player alike. The order is not relevant and should only be interpreted as a list.

1. High repetition
2. Correct completion
3. From easy to difficult
4. Regularity
5. The players should complete the drills in a relaxed condition.
6. Develop up to competitive exercises.
7. Small groups
8. Good demonstration
9. Individualize (coach strengths and weaknesses)
10. Correction, work in detail
11. Adequate material (balls, etc.)
12. Precision before pass strength
13. Increase tempo (from slow to fast)
14. Position specific
15. Variation
16. Train both feet.
17. Show alternatives.
18. Train according to age and developmental stage.
19. When possible, include in all training sessions.
20. Tactic and skills training should be separated from one another .
21. Be aware of training conditions (weather, field, etc) and organize the exercises accordingly.
22. Fun
23. From isolated skill to complex (first simple passing exercises, later passing combinations).
24. Compliment and criticize
25. Include time, space, opponent and partner activity level in the passing exercise once it has been mastered.
26. An exercise should have 100-150 repetitions, until the techniques are automated within the player.

Technical Guide Book

Suggestions and criteria for different techniques (i.e. ball control, ball skills, juggling techniques, dribbling, feints, passes, etc.)

1 General aspects

2 Aspects of good coaching

3 Implementing technique and posture for dribbling
3.1 General implementations
3.2 Implementing technique and posture for instep dribbling
3.3 Implementing technique and posture for dribbling with the inside of the foot
3.4 Implementing technique and posture for dribbling with the outside of the foot

4 Techniques for ball control and ball skills
4.1 Implementing technique and posture for numerous changes in direction/feints and ball techniques
4.2 Implementing technique and posture for pulling the ball back with the sole and the inside of the foot while changing directions
4.3 Implementing technique and posture while doing fast steps on the ball
4.4 Implementing technique and posture while doing a 360-degree turn
4.5 Implementing technique and posture whilst cutting

5 Implementing technique and posture for ball control
5.1 Implementing technique and posture for receiving and controlling the ball
5.2 Implementing technique and posture for controlling the ball with the sole

6 Implementing technique and posture for juggling
6.1 Implementing technique and posture for juggling with the foot/knee/thigh
6.2 Implementing technique and posture for juggling with the head
6.3 Implementing technique and posture for juggling with the heel and the outside of the foot

7 Implementing technique and posture for feints
7.1 Implementing technique and posture for shooting feints
7.2 Implementing technique and posture for the Okocha trick
7.3 Implementing technique and posture for the step-over and the half step-over
7.4 Implementing technique and posture for the pirouette

8 Passing and shooting techniques
8.1 General implementation
8.2 Implementing technique and posture for passing and shooting techniques
- 8.2.1 Stretch shot
- 8.2.2 Spinning
- 8.2.3 Kick with the inside of the foot
- 8.2.4 Pass with the inside of the foot
- 8.2.5 Using the outside of the foot
- 8.2.6 Dropkick
- 8.2.7 Volley shot

1. General aspects

While explaining an exercise, a coach should follow these specific methods:

1. The group stands before the coach.
2. Explain the exercise by splitting up the different sequences of movement. First face the group, and then turn around showing the players the exercise from behind. It will help them reproduce the movements better.
3. The children can repeat the exercise while standing still. Use this time to correct and explain details.
4. Let the children do the exercise in slow motion, then correct mistakes.
5. Increase the pace all the way to maximum speed.
6. Always be sure that all exercises are done with both feet.
7. Short and fast contacts with the ground. Demand short and fast steps.
8. Be sure that the trained patterns of movement grow into a fast and fluent overall motion.

2. Aspects of good coaching

- Always demand accuracy and pace (the slow version does not lead to the necessary success in the game).
- Explaining the exercises should not lead to an information overload (lack of concentration leads to additional mistakes). It is important to find the right balance between correcting and allowing the exercises to flow.
- Players should learn (as in the game) to observe and then implement what they observed.
- Always correct the mistakes to assure they do not become a habit.
- Always address the players with clarity and empathy.
- Advanced groups can be approached simulating game-related stress situations (loud speech, critical comments during the exercise, etc.).
- Always demand full concentration.
- The coach's demeanor (body language, tone of voice, corrections) are a key factor to the quality of the training.

3. Implementing technique and posture for dribbling

3.1 General implementations

- At the beginning of the dribbling, the upper body is slightly leaning forward. When stopping the ball and pulling it back, the upper body is raised a little.
- When applying a body feint, the center of the body typically shifts when the upper body is bent one way or another.
- Do not lean back.
- The elbows are bent at the sides of the body as is typical for walking and running.
- Bend the leg while controlling a ball.
- The ball is touched softly ("tenderly"). Sensitivity for the ball needs to be developed.
- The eyes need to be directed away from the ball regularly (eyes alternate between ball and path ahead).
- Keep up the pace.
- As many touches on the ball as possible.
- The legs are slightly bent at the knee during execution.
- Close ball control (the ball should not leave the foot by more than 50 cm).

3.2 Implementing technique and posture for dribbling and full stretch shots

- The angle of the foot is open.

- The leg is angled.
- The ball is only touched lightly (refined technique).
- Go around the ball when direction is changed.
- The upper body is bent forward.
- Eyes move alternating between the ball and the path ahead.
- No touches with inside – or outside of foot.
- Helps refining the technique, shows how to open the angle of the foot to improve the shooting technique for volleys, shots with the inside of the foot or full stretch shots.

3.3 Implementing technique and posture dribbling with the inside of the foot

- The foot is turned in slightly.
- Toes point up slightly.
- The ball gets a little spin.
- Changing position of the upper body between upright and leaning forward.
- When the ball is controlled with the right foot, the player slightly turns left and vice versa.

3.4 Implementing technique and posture for dribbling with the outside of the foot

- The angle of the foot is slightly turned outward and opened up.
- The ball is touched with the front part of the outside of the foot mainly and also a little with the top (no more than the outside three toes).
- The toes are slightly pushed downward.
- The ball receives a little spin.
- Alternating position of the upper body between upright and leaning forward.
- If the ball is controlled with the right foot, the player can turn right and vice versa.
- The appropriate skill for a linear dribbling at a fast pace.
- If the ball is received with the outside of the foot, the upper body is slightly turned inward. The foot is also slightly turned inward. The angle of the foot is open.

4. Techniques for ball control and ball skills

4.1 Implementing technique and posture for numerous changes in direction/feints/ball techniques

In general:

Feints are body fakes. The motions of the upper body are important. Exercises should always be done with both feet. Use many contacts, keeping the ball close so that the opponent can't get to it.

Tip:

The aim is to get past the opponent and to leave him behind which is why we increase our speed after the move (short 2-3m sprint). Start slowly, increasing speed during the exercise. To help get a feint into the player's system, always correct mistakes, point and explain. Constant repetition with many touches on the ball is the key for players to learn feints and moves.

Set up:

1. Group faces the coach.
2. Explain the exercise and its motion by breaking it down into its elements. First face the group, and then place them so that the players can see the exercise from behind for better comprehension.
3. Let children repeat the exercise while standing, then correct mistakes and explain the exercise in detail.

4. Let children repeat the exercise slowly, then correct mistakes.
5. Increase the pace constantly until at maximum speed.
6. Cones stand in as opponents. To help with the timing, begin the move approx. 2m before you reach the obstacle.
7. It is generally not only the technical quality of a feint that allows it to be successful. The proper timing of when to initiate the feint (not too soon and not too late) is also highly relevant. If two players approach each other at a high speed, the move is made at approx. 3-4m distance. If the player running with the ball approaches a waiting player, the distance is only about 2m.
8. It is important that a visible fake movement of the upper body goes along with each feint. That is what the defender usually reacts to.

4.2 Implementing technique and posture for pulling the ball back with the sole and the inside of the foot while changing directions

- When the ball is pulled back, the supporting leg (left) is at the level of the ball.
- The angle to flick behind the supporting leg with the inside of the foot has to be open and the toes must point downward.
- The foot points inward at 90 degrees.
- The supporting leg moves to the side as well.
- The foot blocks the ball so that the opponent can't get to it.
- After completion we turn 180 degrees and finish the run into the opposite direction.
- Most players play the ball with the sole alone and forget to turn the ankle to cover the ball.
- If the feint is done with the left foot, it is followed by a right turn and vice versa.
- To start the following sprint, the player pushes himself off with the balls of his feet.

4.3 Implementing technique and posture while doing fast steps on the ball

- The upper body is upright at first and then leans over the ball slightly.
- Do not lean back.
- Touch the ball with the soles or the balls of the foot.
- The ball is alternately touched with the right and the left foot. No breaks in between.
- We want a fast and fluent motion.
- Bend the leg.
- Just one step in between (left foot touches ground, right foot the ball).
- Don't play the ball with the inside of the foot.
- Short ground contacts only.
- Ground contact only with the balls of the foot. Not with the entire foot.

4.4 Implementing technique and posture while doing a 360-degree turn

- The turn should be done in a small space.
- The turn and controlling of the ball is one fluent motion.
- There may never be more than 70 cm between the ball and the foot.
- The supporting leg is never more than 50cm away from the ball and moves at a radius of no more than 70cm.
- The upper body is slightly leaning forward. The legs are not far from each other.
- The leg with the foot touching the ball is bent.

4.5 Implementing technique and posture whilst cutting

- Keep the ball close when dribbling (ball should never leave the foot more than 50cm).
- The dribbling should continue as long as possible. Just 1 or 2 meters before the opponent, the direction is changed through cutting inside or outside.

- When cutting inside, the active leg is led from the outside to the inside toward the ball.
- When cutting outside, the moving leg is led from inside to the outside toward the ball.
- See that players put in a 2 to 3m sprint after cutting to shake off the opponent.

5. Implementing technique and posture for ball control

5.1 Implementing technique and posture for receiving and controlling the ball

- Receiving and controlling the ball should never need more than one touch.
- The ball can either be received with the right or the left, the inside or the outside of the foot.
- The ball has to be controlled by the player the moment it touches the ground. If done properly, the ball does not bounce away and can be controlled by the player directly.
- To avoid the ball bouncing away and to assure a fluid and fast ball reception and control, the player has to have good timing and the right technique to control the ball.
- Using the example of ball reception and control with the inside of the right foot, the motion looks like the player needs to control the ball with the inside of his foot the moment it touches the ground. For this the leg is swung from right to left into the direction of the ball. The foot is led downwards toward the ball (similar to the motion when shooting with just the swing being smaller) stopping the ball from bouncing away. The entire weight of the body is now placed on the left supporting leg; the upper body is turned right from the hip (right shoulder turned back). The eyes are on the ball which brings the body to lean over the ball as well.
- When receiving and controlling the ball with the outside of the foot, the angle of the foot is opened. The lower leg is bent inward at the knee as well so that the motion of the foot can go from top to bottom towards the right and towards the ball. The ball is struck with the entire outside of the foot.

Alternative:

Ball reception and control from behind the supporting leg toward the left foot. This receiving technique connects the reception with an immediate change in directions to the side. This technique is done with the inside of the foot. It happens with one touch and is fluid. The foot is turned into the direction of the approaching ball. Just before contact is made, the foot is pulled back (just a little slower than the speed of the ball). Now the ball can be received slowly and controlled with the inside at the same time.

5.2 Implementing technique and for controlling the ball with the sole

For this implementation, the toes of the foot with which the ball is received are pulled up so that when the ball touches the ground, the foot partially covers the ball, stopping it from bouncing up. The leg with which the ball is received is slightly moved forward and bent at the knee. The upper body stays upright; the arms are to the left and right of the body and are bent at the elbows (similar to when carrying cases of water bottles). The palms are pointing at each other.

6. Implementing technique and posture for juggling

6.1 Implementing technique and posture for juggling with the foot/knee/thigh

- When juggling with the knee/thigh, knee and thigh need to be at a 90 degree-angle and the upper body is alternately leaning forward and back.
- The toes are slightly pulled up with most touches. That is how the ball is kept close to the body, receiving a small rotation towards the body. However, one needs less refined technique for it. We therefore suggest juggling with a fully stretched foot.

- We juggle with a fully stretched foot. The angle of the foot needs to be open.
- Always alternate between both feet.
- The upper body is upright and the eyes are pointing downward.
- The supporting leg is slightly bent at the knee.
- The active leg is also bent at the knee. The knee is pulled up slightly so that the foot leaves the ground.
- Contact with the ball is made at about 20cm to 30cm above the ground.
- The arms are to the sides of the body and bent at the elbows (similar to when carrying cases of water bottles).
- The ball should not turn during juggling (logo always visible) => extending the foot here is a good idea. The toes should not be pulled up towards the body; the sole of the foot is parallel to the ground. Use both feet! Set objectives. When objective is reached, set new ones: (10 done, now 12 etc.)

If the level of the group is low, juggling techniques can be introduced the following way:

1. The ball may be taken into the hands in the beginning. Then the ball is dropped onto the right foot and volleyed – catch. Ball is dropped onto the left foot, volleyed and caught, etc.
2. Without hands. The ball may bounce on the ground once between contacts. Right foot – bounce – left foot – bounce, etc.
3. Without bouncing.
4. Increased difficulties:
   (a) Left foot, right foot, left knee, right knee
   (b) Foot, head, knee
   (c) Foot, knee, shoulder, head, shoulder, knee, foot

6.2 Implementing technique and posture for juggling with the head

- For this exercise the player must lean his head back so that the ball can bounce upward off of the forehead.
- Contact with the ball is made with the forehead.
- The player moves into a hollow back, the eyes always on the ball.
- The arms are to sides of the body and bent at the elbows (similar to when carrying cases of water bottles).
- The closing of the eyes before the ball touches the forehead is instinctive and normal.
- The legs are slightly bent at the knees. Through the loose movements coming from the calf muscles, the head is moved upwards towards the ball before the ball touches the forehead. This way the ball bounces off upwards.
- Make sure that the impulse of the calf muscle is not sent out too soon because the effect will otherwise be that the speed is taken out of the ball and it will not be able to bounce upward. Also see that the impulse is not too strong since the ball will otherwise bounce away too far and will be harder to control.

6.3 Implementing technique and posture for juggling with the heel and the outside of the foot

- To be able to play the ball with his heel, after he's played the ball with his foot, the player must take a quick step forward to be able to place the supporting leg in front of the ball. This way he can be sure that the other leg, of which he will now use the heel to play the ball, is in the right position. To then actually play the ball, he needs to bend his supporting leg to be able to turn the body so that the heel can be used. After that he moves back into the original position.
- The eyes are always on the ball.

- Since the heel only offers a small surface with which to play the ball, the player has to be sure to connect with the center of the heel.
- To play the ball with the outside of the foot, the knee must be angled toward the outside. The upper body is alternating between an upright position and one leaning slightly to the side toward the opposite direction. The angle of the foot is opened towards the outside.

7. Implementing technique and posture for feints

7.1 Implementing technique and posture for shooting feints

The shooting feint is a body fake. For that reason it is essential that the player's motion is lunged at the very last possible moment. Shortly before the foot touches the ball, the player begins his feint. To do this, he leads his active leg over the ball, places it on the ground shortly to control the ball with the outside of his foot, taking it to the side. If he does the feint with his right foot, he leads his leg from right to left over the ball, taking the ball with him with the outside of his right foot. The upper body needs to be tilted to the side (it's a move the opponent is supposed to follow) and the arm is moved as if ready to shoot. The supporting leg is pointing forward and not off to the side. It really is no more than stepping over the ball at high speed.

Suggestions shooting feints + pulling the ball behind the supporting leg:

The player begins with dribbling and pretends to take a shot with the right foot. To do this he steps in front of the ball with his left supporting leg and plays the ball to the left with the inside of the right foot. Now he does a 90-degree turn to the left and dribbles past his opponent with the outside of his left foot.

Suggestions shooting feints + cutting inside:
The player swings his active leg over the ball as if about to shoot. Then he plays the ball to the side with the same motion, either with the inside or the outside of the foot taking it past the opponent either left or right at an angle of about 90 degrees. The supporting leg is in front of the ball.

7.2 Implementing technique and posture for the Okocha trick

- The player dribbles with the ball. While dribbling, the ball is wedged in between the feet. The feet are positioned so that the front foot touches the ball at the heel and the hind foot touches it with the inside. The moment both feet make contact with the ball, the ball is pushed onto the heel with the inside of the hind foot. Now the heel is lead upward in a fast abrupt motion. That is how the ball is launched upward and forward. The impulse has to be strong enough so that the ball goes over the opponent's head while running, landing behind him. The player can now control the ball and continue his run.
- The pace may not be slowed down during implementation.
- The upper body is twisted at the hip while the ball is launched upward (the player looks behind himself over his shoulder towards the ball).
- After practicing the broken down feint (without opponent), we practice it against a cone, then against a passive defender and finally against an active defender.
- When practicing with an opponent, the ball is lifted over the opponent and over the player doing the exercise.
- The ball needs to be controlled immediately after the feint in order to shake off the opponent with a sprint.

7.3 Implementing technique and posture for the step-over/ half step-over

The player begins his run with the outside of his right foot and leads the right foot from the inside to the outside right over or around the ball. He then also pulls the left leg over the ball and plays it to the left with the outside of the left foot, dribbling past the opponent.

Alternative:

- First practice it without an opponent.
- Practice the motion sequence while standing still.
- Practice the motion sequence while moving.
- Place a cone for an opponent.
- Remember to also use your weak foot.

Suggestions:

- The step-over is a body feint. This means that if the feint is intended for the right, the upper body has to lean right while the ball is led to the left.
- The aim is to trick the opponent with the upper body and to get him to follow the move. The player on the ball gains time which he needs to use in order to get past the opponent.
- The player needs to move on the balls of his feet.
- At the beginning of the motion, the player should avoid long and big jumps and instead focus on fast and short movements with the upper body and the leg which is led over the ball to the right.
- First the exercise is done slowly and without an opponent. Then the pace is increased and a cone is added as an obstruction. Finally the feint is practiced in a one-on-one situation.
- Short and fast motions.
- Eyes are not only on the ball but also on the path ahead.
- After implementation, the ball is controlled a little to the left with the outside of the foot.
- Short and fast steps.

The difference between a step-over and a half step-over is that for the step over the foot goes all the way around the ball while for the half step-over the motion is only suggested.

7.4 Implementing technique and posture for the pirouette

- The player begins with dribbling. If he starts with the right foot, he lifts the leg up and the knee makes a 90-degree angle. He now touches the ball with the sole of his right foot, turns 180 degrees to the left (left shoulder points to the back) and places the right foot to the left of the ball (his back to the opponent). With his second touch, the ball is pulled back with the sole of the left foot (left leg equally angled as mentioned above) for another 180-degree turn. Now the player is in the starting position again. Following this order of motion, the left leg is placed to the left of the ball and the ball is controlled and taken to the right with the outside of the right foot.
- Turn into the opponent sprinting to the side away from him.
- Start slowly.
- The hand can touch the respective shoulder indicating the desired direction.
- Fast and fluid motion.

8. Passing and shooting technique

8.1 General implementations

- The supporting leg should be 30 – 40cm next to the ball.
- The upper body is slightly leaning over the ball.
- The foot is swung downwards.

- The player awaiting the pass approaches the passing player and receives the pass while going forward towards the ball. He receives it with one touch or passes it on immediately.
- The pass needs to be played into the path of the player awaiting the ball.
- The player passing has to consider the path of the player awaiting the ball.
- The first movement of the player receiving the pass occurs when the passer takes aim.
- The pass beating the opponent should be played to the correct side. Should a player want to pass to the left of the opponent, he should play a curve around the opponent with the inside of his left foot. If he uses the inside of his right foot to pass to the left instead, the ball is easily intercepted or the path is forced to the side rather than into deep space.
- Due to the high demands on a player's refined technique, the pace of the pass should always be adjusted to the level of the players (children and beginners can start slowly).

8.2 Implementing technique and posture for passing and shooting techniques

Intensity of the pass or the shot, accuracy and timing are significant factors for a successful shot or pass.

Explanations for different shooting techniques:

8.2.1 Stretch shot

- Tip of the foot points downwards, ankle is tight.
- The arms are positioned as if passing: Shooting with the right stretch, the left arm goes towards the right hip, shooting with the left stretch, the right arm goes to the left hip.
- To illustrate, let the players kick in the air with all their power. What do the arms do?

8.2.2 Spinning

- The ball is played with the tip of the inside of the foot, giving it a spin. The body leans to the side.

8.2.3 Kick with the inside of the foot

- The ball is played with the inside and with the stretch. The supporting leg is next to the ball and the player's upper body leans to the side. The toes point downward similar to when taking a stretch shot.

8.2.4 Pass with the inside of the foot

- The tip of the foot points up, the ankle is tight and opened up 90 degrees to the outside. The active leg is slightly lifted and the ball is struck in the center. The body leans over the ball without going into a hollow back.

8.2.5 Using the outside of the foot

- When playing the ball with the outside of the foot, leaning back slightly is allowed. The ball is played with the outside toes and outside of the foot, giving it a spin.

8.2.6 Dropkick

- For the dropkick, the ball is struck with the stretch. This is done the moment the ball hits the ground.
- We take the ball into our hands, extend the arms, drop the ball. The moment the ball touches the ground it needs to be struck with the stretch. The leg swings through after contact is made. The ball should not turn.
  Problems with the dropkick:
  The ball may be struck too soon, before it touches the ground. => demonstrate and explain.
- Ball is struck too late, after it has touched the ground and is back on its way up. => demonstrate and explain.

- This exercise may be difficult for some children requiring patience until the motion sinks in. It may help to allow the child to kick past the ball when it touches the ground. This way the child can get the right feeling/ timing for the moment the ball needs to be struck without having to chase after the ball each time. It may also help to point out the right moment by calling out a word at the proper moment. This exercise makes sense to perform in front of a fence.

8.2.7 Volley shot

- For the volley shot, the entire body should lean forward slightly and the ball should be struck low. The ball receives more pressure and accuracy that way.

Suggestions for corrections by the coach:

- Strike the ball before the supporting leg.
- Swing through after making contact.
- Tip of the foot points towards the ground.
- Ankle is tight.
- Watch the position of the arms.
- Small steps towards the ball.

Legend:

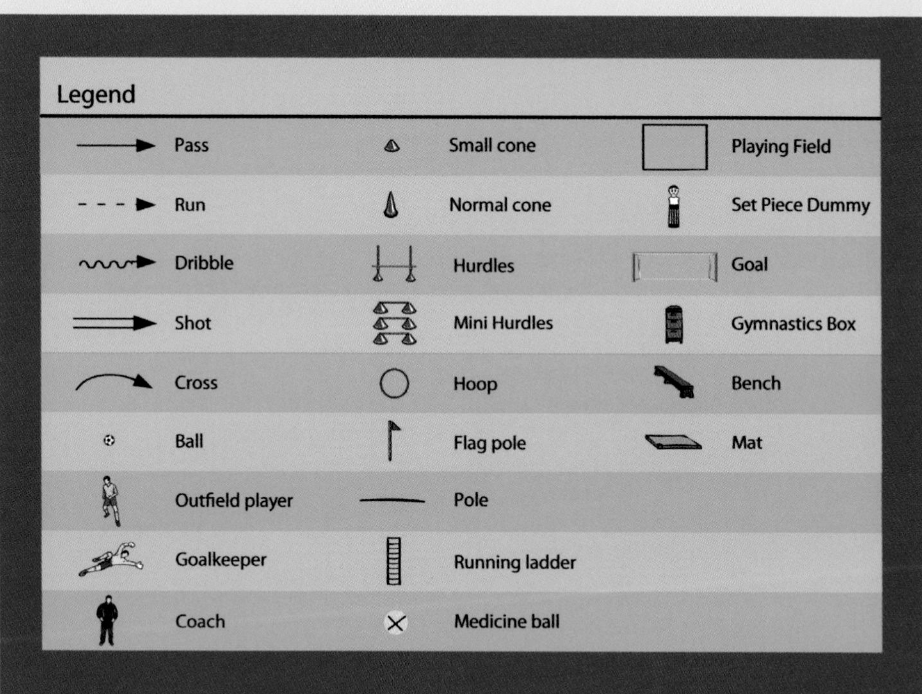

1 "Stroking" Ball with the Sole – Side-on

Training Target
- **Ball skill (Touch on the ball)**

Training Emphasis
- **Dribbling control**
- **Fitness program**

Training Aspects

Skills involved:	**Leaping strength, Control, Trapping into space, Dribbling, Inside of the foot, Combining technical skill with movement, Running technique with/without ball**
Age level:	**6-8 years, 9-12 years, 13-14 years, 15 years to Adult**
Level of play:	**Recreational, Advanced**
Type of training:	**Individual training, Group training**
Training structure:	**Warm-up, Progression**
Purpose:	**Improve individual qualities**
Total number of players:	**2 or more players**
Participating players:	**Whole team**
Training location:	**Any**
Spatial awareness:	**Limited playing field**
Duration:	**1 min**
Physiology:	**Soccer-specific endurance**

Organization:
Marked-out box.

Implementation:
The player moves the ball at the side of his body, i.e. to the right with his right foot and to the left with his left foot. The ball is controlled in such a way as to cause a slight dummy movement. The first touch of the ball is with the sole. The foot is then moved sideways over the ball so that the ball "wanders" over the whole sole. The sideways movement causes the legs to cross. When the ball is moved with the right foot, the right foot is on the left of the left (supporting) foot. This automatically leads to a slight turning in the hips (the left shoulder turns to the right).

Note:
- "Stroking" the ball means dribbling while only lightly touching the ball.
- Keep the legs flexed.
- On the soles of the feet.
- Quick feet.
- The upper body should be slightly leaning forwards.
- Don't lean back.
- The arms should be kept at the side of the body in their normal positions when running/walking.
- Players should keep their head up and an eye on the ball.
- Keep the speed up.
- As many touches as possible.

Field size:
Depending upon number of players, vary between 5-30 m.

Distance between the cones:
Depending upon number of players.
Calculation: 12 player = 10 x 15 m.

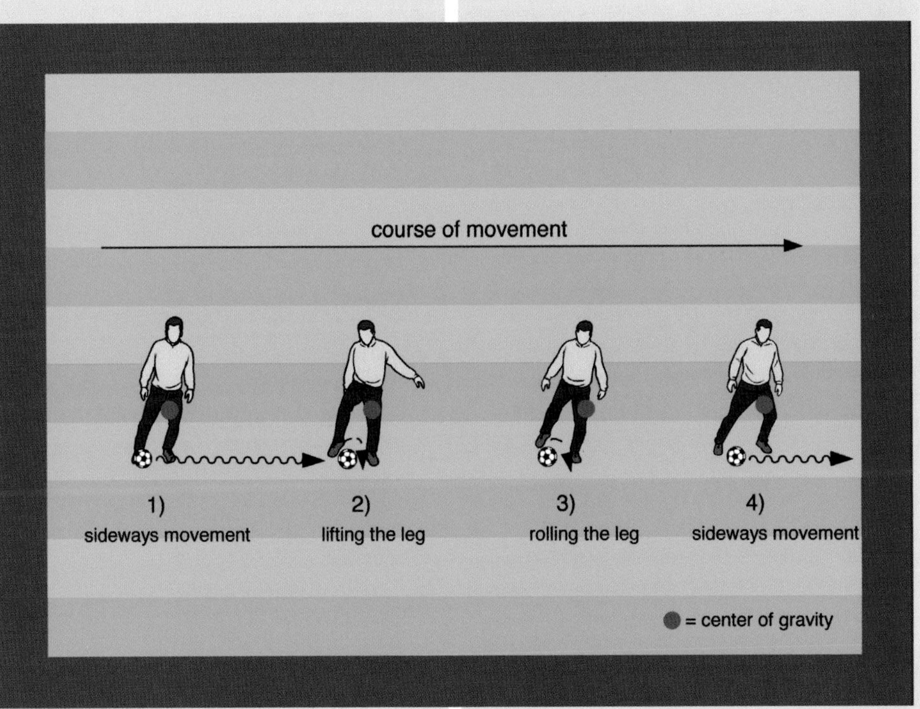

2 Alternating Pulling the Ball Back and Forth with the Right and Left Instep

Training Target
- Ball skill (Touch on the ball)

Training Emphasis
- Finesse on the ball
- Fitness program

Training Aspects	
Skills involved:	Leaping strength, Control, Flexibility, Soccer-specific endurance, Inside of the foot, Combining technical skill with movement, Speed power
Age level:	6-8 years, 9-12 years, 13-14 years, 15 years to Adult
Level of play:	Recreational
Type of training:	Individual training, Team training
Training structure:	Warm-up, Progression
Purpose:	Improve individual qualities, Willpower training
Total number of players:	2 or more players
Participating players:	Whole team
Training location:	Any
Spatial awareness:	Limited playing field, Penalty box
Duration:	1 min
Physiology:	Soccer-specific endurance, Strength endurance, Power & Speed

Organization:
Enclosed field. One ball per player.

Implementation:
The player plays the ball alternately from his left to right instep. He should try to move the ball as fast as possible and at the same time take his eye off the ball. The trainer can take the player's eyes off the ball by calling or signaling to him. The coach can hold up different numbers of fingers. The player should call out the number of fingers being shown.
As soon as the ball leaves the left foot, that foot becomes the supporting foot (the center of gravity switches from the right to the left foot) as soon as the ball leaves the right foot, that foot becomes the supporting foot. The ball permanently moving back and forth also causes the center of gravity to switch back and forth.

Note:
- Keep the legs flexed.
- On the soles of the feet.
- Quick feet.
- Don't touch the ball with the whole instep, if possible only with the ball of the foot.
- The upper body should be slightly leaning forwards.
- Don't lean back.
- Arms flexed and moving against the direction of movement.
- Players should keep their head up and have an eye on the ball when receiving the ball.
- Keep the speed up.
- As many touches as possible.
- The ball should be played side-on in the middle of the ball.

Field size:
A box which could vary in size from between 5-30 m, depending upon group size.

Distance between the cones:
Depending upon group size 5-30 m.

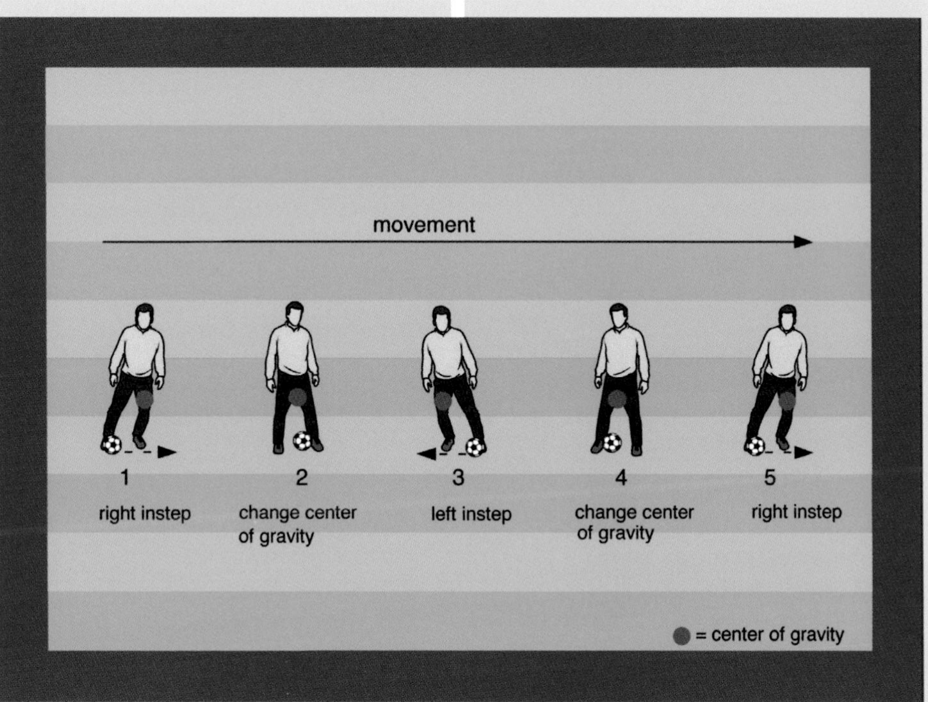

3 Moving the Ball Right and Left with the Sole of the Foot Forwards, Backwards and Sideways

Training Target
- **Endurance**
- **Ball skill (Touch on the ball)**

Training Emphasis
- **Finesse on the ball**
- **Fitness program**

Training Aspects

Skills involved:	Leaping strength, Control, Flexibility, Combining technical skill with movement
Age level:	Any age
Level of play:	Advanced
Type of training:	Individual training, Team training
Training structure:	Warm-up, Progression
Purpose:	Improve individual qualities, Willpower training
Total number of players:	2 or more players
Participating players:	Whole team
Training location:	Any
Spatial awareness:	Limited playing field
Duration:	1 min
Physiology:	Soccer-specific endurance, Strength endurance, Power & Speed

Organization:
Using 4 cones, lay out a field suitable to the number of players. Each player has a ball.

Implementation:
The player dribbles the ball with the sole of his foot. The player is free to choose which direction he moves in. The direction can also be given by the coach (forwards, backwards, right, left).

Note:
- The ball should be played "softly." The player should develop a feel for the ball.
- Make it clear to the player that the foot is not in contact with the ball for very long and the foot doesn't move over the whole ball.
- The upper body should be alternately over the ball and slightly leaning forwards.
- The arms should be kept at the side of the body in their normal positions when running/walking.
- The legs should be slightly bent at the knees.
- The ground should be alternately touched with the balls of the feet.
- The players should keep their heads up and not look at the ball. Suggestion: The coach calls to the player to look at him. Now the coach shows a number with his fingers which the player has to call out.
- The exercise is relatively strenuous due to the permanent switching of the whole body weight onto the supporting foot. This is particularly relevant for children. As a result, the exercise would be completed for a maximum of 1 minute, followed by a short break.

Field size:
Depending upon group size. Calculation: 12 players approx. 10 x 15 m.

Distance between the cones:
10 meters horizontally, 15 m vertically.

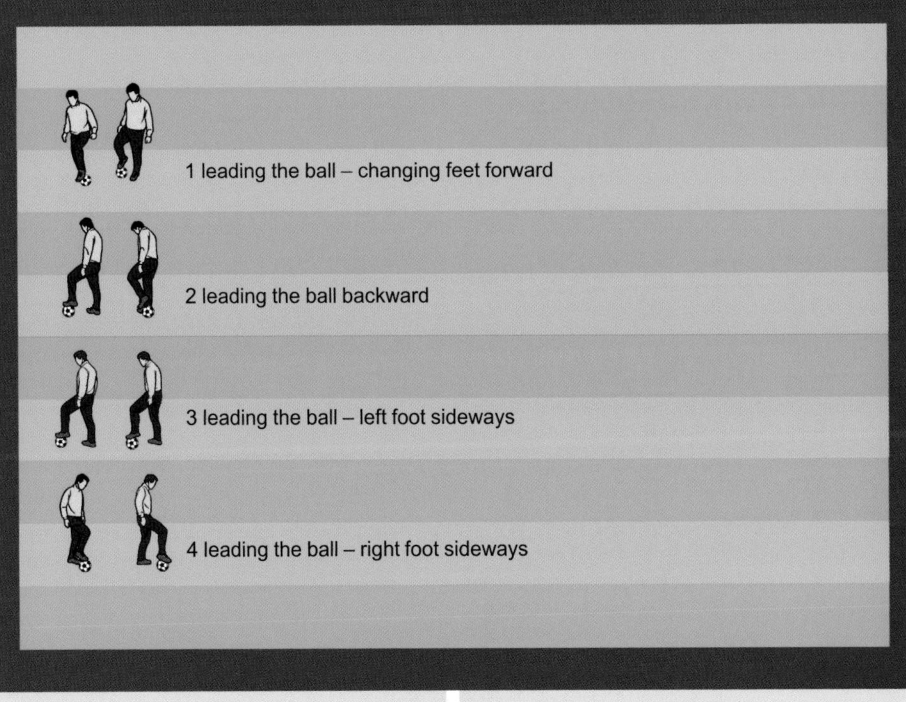

4 "Stepping" with the Ball

Training Target
- **Ball skill (Touch on the ball)**

Training Emphasis
- **Finesse on the ball**
- **Ball control**
- **Fitness program**

Training Aspects

Skills involved:	**Speed of movement with ball, Flexibility, Soccer-specific endurance, Combining technical skill with movement, Speed power**
Age level:	**9-12 years, 13-14 years, 15 years to Adult**
Level of play:	**Recreational**
Type of training:	**Individual training, Group training**
Training structure:	**Warm-up, Progression**
Purpose:	**Improve individual qualities**
Total number of players:	**2-4 players**
Participating players:	**Whole team**
Training location:	**Any**
Spatial awareness:	**Limited playing field, Penalty box**
Duration:	**1 min**
Physiology:	**Soccer-specific endurance, Strength endurance, Power & Speed**

Organization:
One ball per player within the playing area.

Implementation:
The players each have a ball. The players begin to tap on top of the ball, alternately with each foot, with the sole of their feet as quickly as possible. The upper body should be upright and the legs slightly bent at the knees. The players should swing their arms as if they were running to support the alternating leg movement. The ball should be moved forwards or backwards in a straight line during the exercise. Alternative: A variation is that the players use the same technique to move through a small gate with the ball at their feet or to complete the drill in a group. The players should practice keeping their head up and improving their peripheral vision.

Note:
- The upper body should be held upright at the start of the skill and then slightly leant over the ball.
- Don't lean back.
- The ball should be moved with the sole of the foot or the ball of the foot.
- Demonstrate the exercise so that the players watch from behind.
- Start slowly and then increase speed.
- The ball should be tapped alternately with the left and right feet without a pause in between.
- Fluid, fast movements.
- Bend the knees.
- One step between touches, e.g. the player's left foot touches the ground as his right (ball of his) foot makes contact with the ball.
- The player should not touch the ball with their instep.
- Quick feet.
- The players should only touch the ground with the balls of their feet, not with their whole foot.

Field size:
A box which could vary in size from between 5-30 m, depending upon group size.

Distance between the cones:
Depending upon group size 5-30 m.

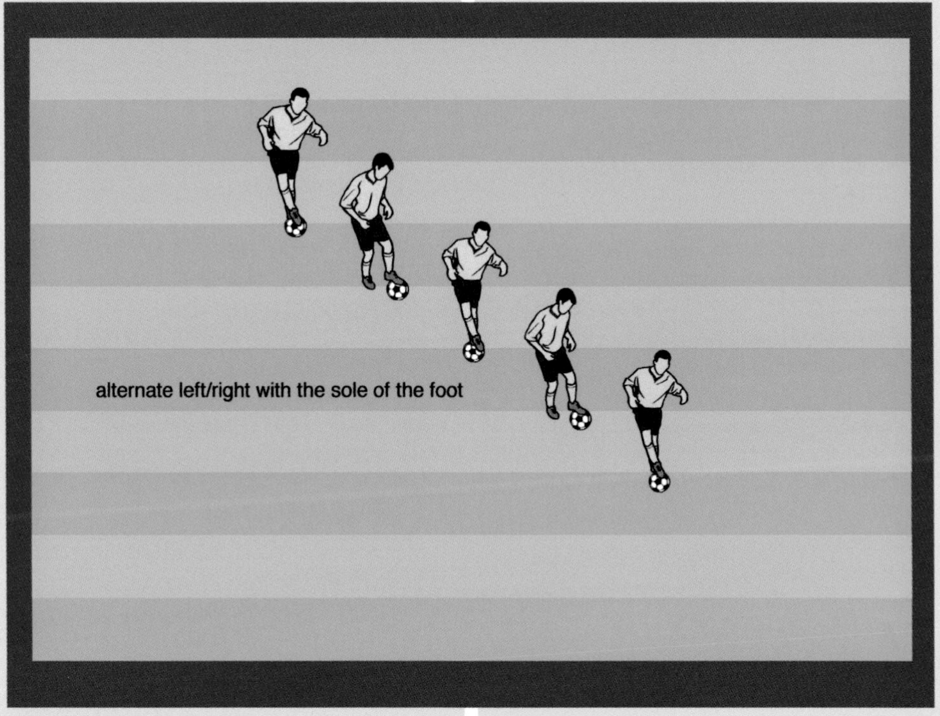

5 Ball Control with the Sole of the Foot

Training Target
- Ball skill (Touch on the ball)

Training Emphasis
- Dribblng control
- Finesse on the ball
- Coordination

Training Aspects

Skills involved:	Speed of movement with ball, Quick anticipation, Control, Trapping into space, Dribbling, Quick decision-making, Quick processing, Inside of the foot, Combining technical skill with movement, Speed in change of direction, Laces
Age level:	Any age
Level of play:	Recreational
Type of training:	Group training, Team training
Training structure:	Warm-up, Conclusion, Progression, Main point/Emphasis
Purpose:	Improve individual qualities
Total number of players:	2 or more players
Participating players:	Whole team
Training location:	Any
Spatial awareness:	Half-field, Penalty box
Duration:	5-10 min
Physiology:	Soccer-specific endurance, Speed endurance, Power & Speed

Organization:
The players split into pairs. One ball for each pair.

Implementation:
One player has the ball, the second player stands behind him. The player without the ball attempts to take the ball from the player in possession. The player with the ball uses his body to protect the ball. He can only move the ball forwards and backwards using the sole of his feet. If player B wins the ball, the roles are reversed. If the player without the ball fails to gain possession within 1 minute, the players change position after the signal from the coach.

Note:
- The player can protect the ball well by using the sole of his feet. If nothing else, the player trying to gain possession can only attack the ball from the side, not from above. The player in possession can also put enough downwards pressure on the ball to ensure that he can even remain in possession when the attacker makes contact with the ball.
- At first the opponent should take a passive roll, so that the player in possession can develop a feel for the "protecting position."
- The opponent should then become live after a couple of dry, passive runs.
- The player should try to make his body as wide as possible to help protect the ball.
- Using the arms too much during the exercise should be stopped by the coach as this would be judged a foul in a game situation and so would lead to loss of possession.

Field size:
Depending upon number of players - in the 18-yard box or in one half.

Distance between the cones:
None

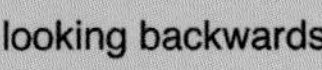

6 Dribbling Instep/Outstep and Laces

Training Target
- **Ball skill (Touch on the ball)**

Training Emphasis
- **Dribbling control**

Training Aspects

Skills involved:	Leaping strength, Outside of the foot, Control, Dribbling, Inside of the foot, Combining technical skill with movement, Laces
Age level:	6-8 years, 9-12 years, 13-14 years, 15-16 years
Level of play:	Recreational
Type of training:	Individual training, Group training
Training structure:	Warm-up, Progression
Purpose:	Improve individual qualities
Total number of players:	2 or more players
Participating players:	Whole team
Training location:	Any
Spatial awareness:	Limited playing field, Penalty box
Duration:	5 min
Physiology:	Soccer-specific endurance

Organization:
One ball per player in a marked field.

Implementation:
The players dribble alternately in the space provided with the instep, outstep and the laces. The players should keep their head up in order to not dribble out of the playing area or to collide with the other players.

Note:
Dribbling laces:
- The ankle should be open.
- The leg flexed.
- The players should use a light touch.
- The player should run around the ball when the direction changes.
- Upper body should be leaning forward.
- Players should keep their head up and an eye on the ball.
- The players should not use the instep or outstep. Particularly children tend to turn their ankle inwards and move the ball with their outstep. The coach should correct the player on this point and ensure that the players' feet remain stable.

Dribbling instep:
- The foot slightly turned inwards.
- Toes lightly turned upwards.
- Ball receives a slight spin.
- The upper body varies between standing upright and slightly leaning forwards.
- If the ball is on the right side, the player runs left and if the ball is on the left side the player runs right. Dribbling outstep-the foot should be lightly turned outwards and downwards.
- The ball should be dribbled with the outstep and a little with the laces (maximum the outer three toes).
- The toes should be slightly turned downwards.
- Ball receives a slight spin.
- The upper body varies between standing upright and slightly leaning forwards.

- If the ball is on the right side, the player runs left and if the ball is on the left side, the player runs right.

Field size:
A box which could vary in size from between 5-30 m, depending upon group size.

Distance between the cones:
Depending upon group size 5-30 m.

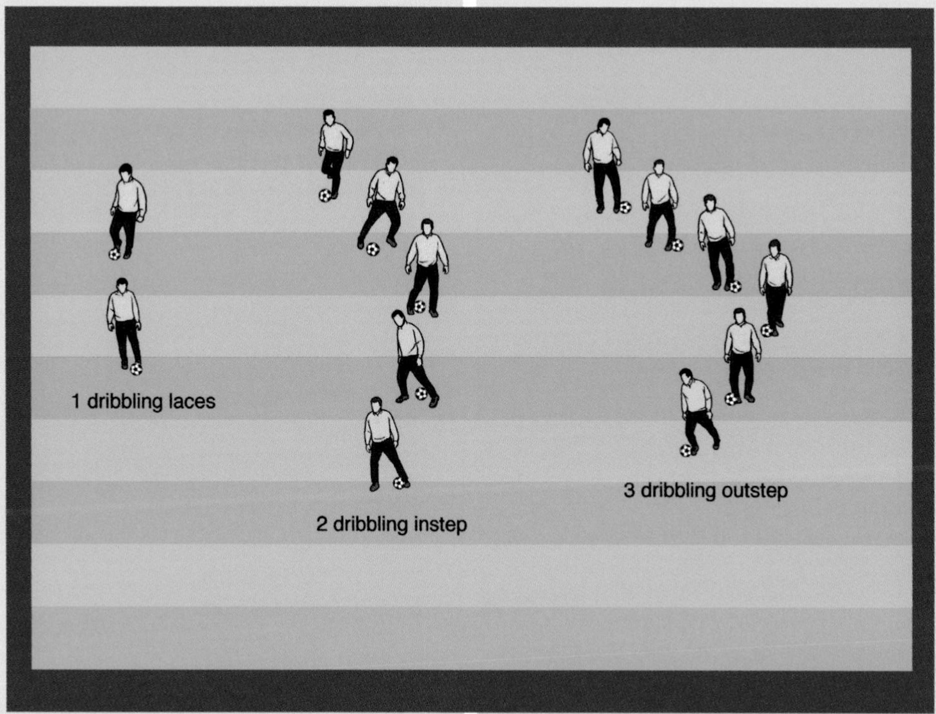

7 Dribbling with 360-Degree Turn

Training Target
- Ball skill (Touch on the ball)

Training Emphasis
- Finesse on the ball

Training Aspects

Skills involved:	Outside of the foot, Trapping into space, Dribbling, Inside of the foot, Combining technical skill with movement
Age level:	6-8 years, 9-12 years, 13-14 years, 15-16 years
Level of play:	Beginner, Advanced
Type of training:	Individual training, Group training
Training structure:	Warm-up, Progression
Purpose:	Improve individual qualities
Total number of players:	2 or more players
Participating players:	Whole team
Training location:	Any
Spatial awareness:	Limited playing field
Duration:	1-10 min
Physiology:	Soccer-specific endurance, Explosiveness, Speed endurance, Power & Speed

Organization:
Set up a box. Depending upon group size the 18-yard box can also be used. One ball per player.

Implementation:
The players dribble with the ball. Upon the call from the coach they turn (360 degrees) and then dribble on. The ball should be kept under close control during the turn. The player must use fewer than 3 touches for the turn. The trick is then followed by a short sprint.

Note:
- The turn should be confined to as small a space as possible.
- The turn with control should be a fluid movement.
- The ball mustn't ever be further than 70 cm from the player's foot.
- The supporting foot should not be further than a 70 cm radius from the ball.
- The upper body should be slightly leaning forward. Both legs are shoulder width apart.
- The leg in possession of the ball should be slightly bent.
- The last touch of the turn is also the first touch of the sprint (explosive sprint out of the turn).

Field size:
Varies, depending upon number of players. Calculation for 12 players: 10 x 15 meters.

Distance between the cones:
Varies depending upon number of players. Calculation for 12 players: 10 meters wide, 15 meters long.

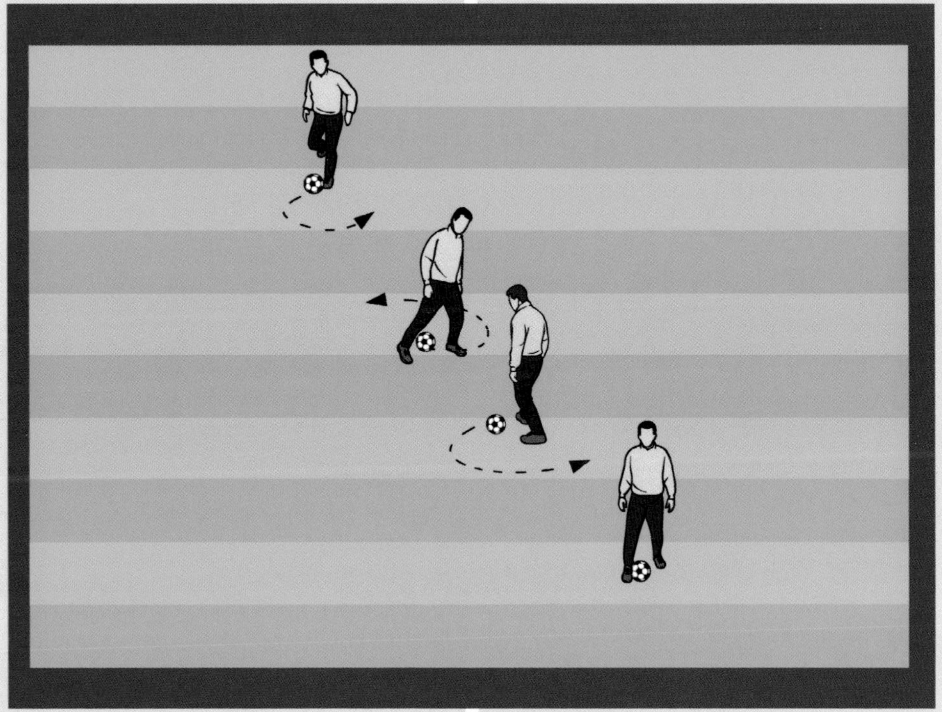

Training Target
- Ball skill (Touch on the ball)

Training Emphasis
- Finesse on the ball
- Feinting/trick dribbling

Training Aspects

Skills involved:	Leaping strength, Speed of movement with ball, Flexibility, Dribbling, Soccer-specific endurance, Bodyfake, Combining technical skill with movement, Speed endurance, Speed power
Age level:	6-8 years, 9-12 years, 13-14 years, 15 years to Adult
Level of play:	Recreational
Type of training:	Individual training, Group training, Team training
Training structure:	Warm-up, Progression
Purpose:	Improve individual qualities
Total number of players:	1-3 players, 4 or more players
Participating players:	Whole team
Training location:	Any
Spatial awareness:	Limited playing field, Penalty box
Duration:	1 min
Physiology:	Soccer-specific endurance, Strength endurance, Speed endurance, Power & Speed

Organization:
Each player has a ball in an enclosed box.

Implementation:
The player starts dribbling with his left foot. Approx. 2 meters in front of the opponent (can also be a cone) he makes a dummy, he moves his center of gravity to the left (upper body goes to the left side/ center of gravity over the left leg). Immediately afterwards he straightens up his upper body again and sprints with the outstep of the other foot past his opponent on the right.

Note:
- The upper body slightly leans forwards at the start of the exercise and should be moved to the side at the end of the trick.
- Don't lean back.
- The left dribbling foot becomes the supporting foot. It would be ideal if the player moved and pushed off from the ball of his left foot.
- Demonstrate the exercise so that the players watch from behind.
- Start slowly and then increase speed.
- Train with both feet.
- The upper body should lean slightly forward at the start of the exercise and then should slightly lean back.
- Fluid, fast movements.
- Player should keep their head up and an eye on the ball when receiving the ball.
- Quick feet.
- Fast, short movements.
- Control and dribble the ball with the outstep.

Field size:
A box which could vary in size from between 5-30 m, depending upon group size.

Distance between the cones:
Depending upon group size 5-30 m.

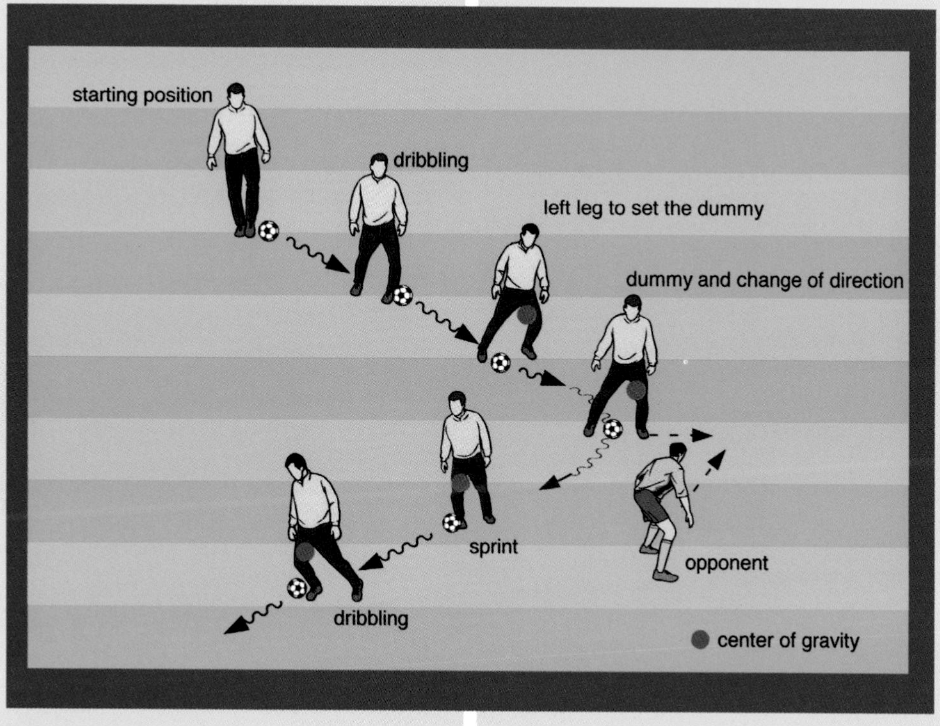

9 Flicking with the Instep/Outstep

Training Target

- **Ball skill (Touch on the ball)**

Training Emphasis

- **Dribbling control**
- **Finesse on the ball**
- **Feinting/trick dribbling**
- **Fitness program**

Training Aspects

Skills involved:	Leaping strength, Speed of movement with ball, Quick anticipation, Outside of the foot, Control, Trapping into space, Dribbling, Quick decision-making, Quick processing, Inside of the foot, Bodyfake, Combining technical skill with movement, Quick understanding of danger
Age level:	6-8 years, 9- 12 years, 13-14 years
Level of play:	Recreational
Type of training:	Group training
Training structure:	Warm-up, Progression
Purpose:	Attack behavior, Improve individual qualities
Total number of players:	3 players, 4 or more players
Participating players:	Whole team
Training location:	Indoor, Asphalt, Turf field, Grass field
Spatial awareness:	Limited playing field
Duration:	5-10 min
Physiology:	Soccer-specific endurance, Fundamental endurance, Speed endurance, Power & Speed, Explosiveness training

Organization:
Where possible, each player should have their own ball. Depending upon the number of players, set up several groups. Opponents can also be substituted with cones. The opponents/cones should be placed to the offset to the side.

Implementation:
The player starts by dribbling to the first opponent/cone. Approx. 1-2 meters in front of the cone he flicks the ball back with the inside of his left foot and sprints past the opponent/cone. He then dribbles to the second opponent/cone. There he flicks the ball back, this time with the inside of his right foot and sprints past the opponent/cone. The second player can start when the first player is at the first cone. The next time through, the players flick the ball first with the inside of their right foot and then with their left foot.

Note:
- Ensure the players use close control when dribbling (the ball shouldn't be further than 50 cm away from the ball.)
- The players should dribble as far as possible. They should only flick the ball (so changing direction of the ball) when 1-2 meters in front of the opponent.
- The players' standing leg should be turned inwards towards the ball when flicking the ball with the instep.
- The players' standing leg should be turned outwards away from the ball when flicking the ball with the outstep.

- Ensure that the players put in a short sprint (2-3 meter) after passing their opponent.

Field size:
8 x 16 m

Distance between the cones:
4 m

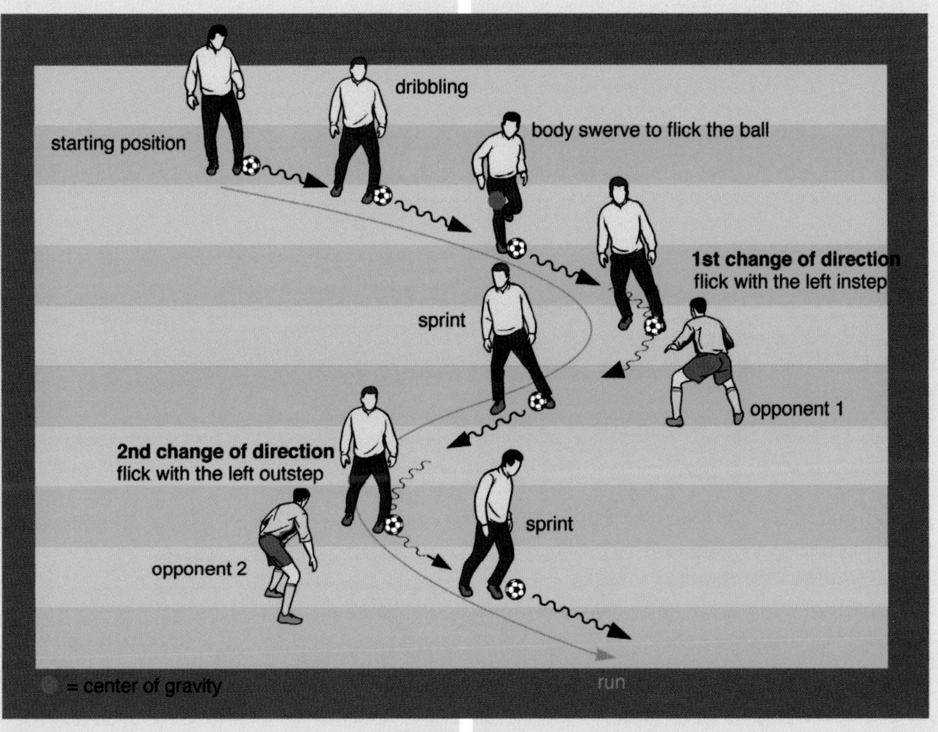

10 Step-over

Training Target
- Ball skill (Touch on the ball)

Training Emphasis
- Finesse on the ball
- Feinting/trick dribbling
- Fitness program
- Coordination

Training Aspects	
Skills involved:	Speed of movement with ball, Quick anticipation, Outside of the foot,, Trapping into space, Flexibility, Dribbling, Quick decision-making, Inside of the foot, Bodyfake, Combining technical skill with movement, Quickness of reaction, Speed in change of direction
Age level:	Any age
Level of play:	Recreational
Type of training:	Individual training, Group training
Training structure:	Warm-up, Progression
Purpose:	Attack behavior, Improve individual qualities
Total number of players:	2 or more players
Participating players:	Whole team
Training location:	Any
Spatial awareness:	Free space
Duration:	1-10 min
Physiology:	Soccer-specific endurance, Power & Speed

Organisation:
The trick can be practiced in a coned-in area or anywhere where the player has some space.

Implementation:
The player starts dribbling the ball with his right outstep and then moves his right foot from left to right over the ball. He then pulls his left leg over the ball in the same manner and knocks the ball with the outside of his left past the opponent.

Alternative:
- First without an opponent.
- Practice the skill standing.
- Practice the skill while in movement.
- Substitute a cone for the opponent.
- Train with both feet.
- Goals which are scored in training, preceded by a step-over, are worth two points.

Note:
- The step-over is a full body action, i.e. the upper body must lean to the right (the opposite direction) while the ball is played to the left.
- The player should attempt to dummy his opponent with the movement of his upper body as much as possible. As a result, the player with the ball can win some time.
- The upper body should be slightly leaning forwards.
- The player should move on the balls of his feet.
- At the start of the trick, the player should not complete a slow, obvious movement,

rather a quick and sudden stepover and upper body swerve.

- Start by training slowly without obstacles or opponents. Then increase the speed and introduce obstacles (cones). Finally train the trick with an opponent.
- Short, sharp movements.
- The players' head should not be down, looking at the ball. The player should try to vary between looking up and at the ball.
- After completing the trick the player should control the ball slightly to one side (left) with the outstep.
- Short, quick sprint. The difference between a stepover and the scissors is that the players' foot is moved over the ball during the stepover and in front of the ball for the scissors.

Field size:
Flexible

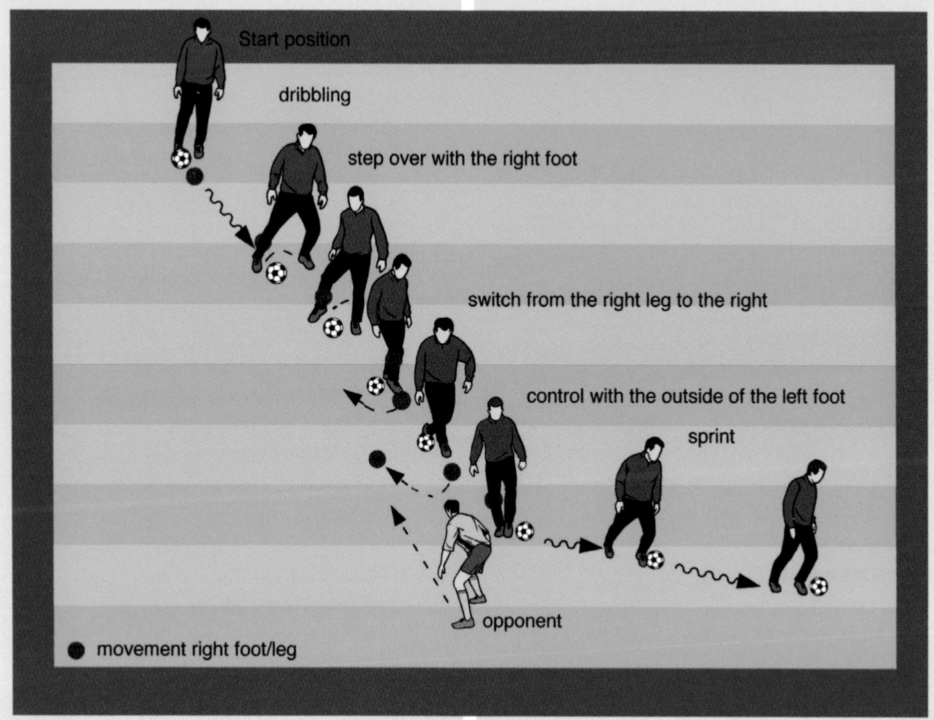

11 Dragging the Ball Back with the Sole of the Foot

Training Target
- **Ball skill (Touch on the ball)**
- **One-on -one training**

Training Emphasis
- **Finesse on the ball**
- **Feinting/trick dribbling**

Training Aspects

Skills involved:	One-on-one, Defensive/Offensive play, Speed of movement with ball, Quick anticipation, Controlling the ball, Quick decision-making, Soccer-specific endurance, Soccer-specific sprint training, Quick processing, Inside of the foot passing, Bodyfake, Combining technical skill with movement, Quickness of reaction, Speed in change of direction, Speed power
Age level:	6-8 years, 9-12 years, 15 years to Adult
Level of play:	Advanced
Type of training:	Small group training 2-6 players
Training structure:	Main point/Emphasis
Purpose:	Defense behavior, Attack behavior, Improve individual qualities
Total number of players:	2 players
Participating players:	Defenders, Midfielders, Forwards
Training location:	Any
Spatial awareness:	Free space
Duration:	5-10 min
Physiology:	Soccer-specific endurance, Strength endurance, Explosiveness, Speed endurance Power & Speed, Explosiveness training

Organization:
2 players, 1 ball

Implementation:
The player dribbles towards his opponent as per the graphic. When he is 2 meters from the player he drags the ball back with the sole of his right foot. He then passes the ball with the instep or the laces of his right foot past his opponent on the right side (on the opponent's left side). He then passes his opponent on the player's right and takes the ball as close behind his opponent as possible. The player's foot is the foot closest to the ball.

Note:
- The supporting foot (left) is next to the ball when dragging the ball back.
- The upper body is slightly leaning over the ball.
- The player squeezes past his opponent at high speed.
- Dragging the ball back and passing with an explosive, curved sprint should be one fluid action.
- Control should be direct, with the first touch.
- The right or left instep can be used, depending upon the direction of the pass.
- The ball should not be passed too hard.
- Precise passing.

Field size:
6 x 15 m

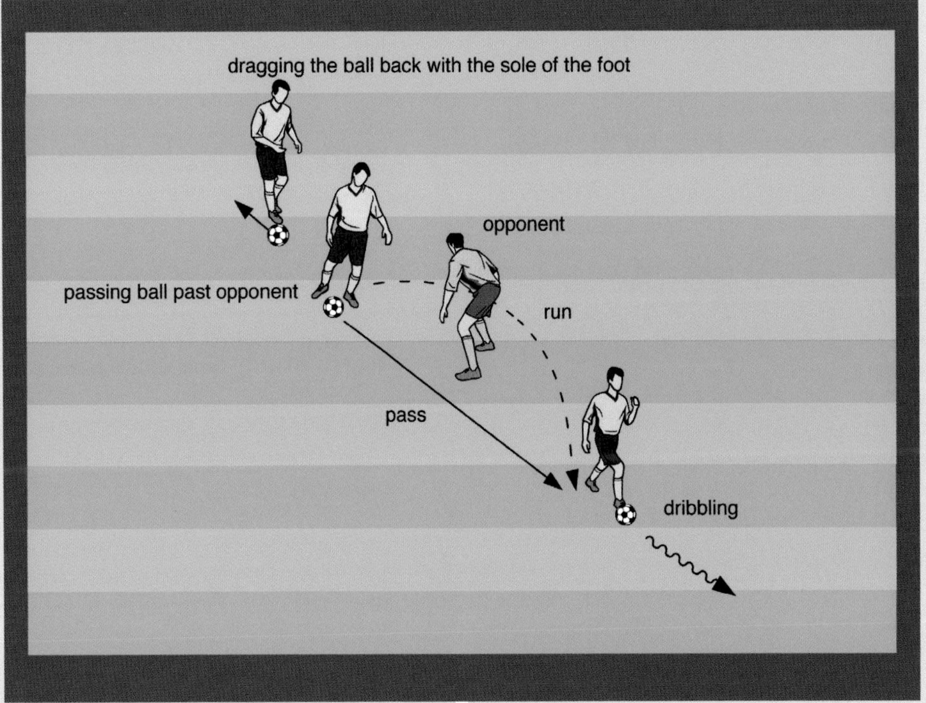

12 American Fake

Training Target
- **Ball skill (Touch on the ball)**

Training Emphasis
- **Finesse on the ball**
- **Feinting/trick dribbling**

Training Aspects

Skills involved:	**Speed of movement with ball, Control Flexibility, Bodyfake, Combining technical skill with movement**
Age level:	**Any age**
Level of play:	**Recreational**
Type of training:	**Individual training, Group training**
Training structure:	**Warm-up, Progression**
Purpose:	**Improve individual qualities**
Total number of players:	**1-3 players, 4 or more players**
Participating players:	**Whole team**
Training location:	**Any**
Spatial awareness:	**Limited playing field**
Duration:	**1-10 min**
Physiology:	**Soccer-specific endurance**

Organization:
Set up a coaching area suitable to the number of players. The 18-yard box could also be used

Implementation:
The player dribbles forwards with the ball, stops, then drags the ball behind his supporting foot with the sole of his foot. He then turns his ankle inwards so that the ball is covered by the ball and passes the ball with the instep in the opposite direction (backwards). If the player completes this skill with his right foot, then he turns round his left supporting foot.

Note:
- The upper body should slightly leaning forward at the start of the exercise and should be straightened somewhat when controlling and dragging back the ball. Don't lean back.
- The ankle which drags the ball back with the instep, and the toes, should point towards the floor.
- The ankle should be turned 90 degrees inwards.
- The supporting foot also moves to the side.
- The foot covers the ball, so that the opponent can't play the ball.
- Upon completion the player has turned 180 degrees and then dribbles in the opposite direction (back).
- Most players pass the ball with the sole of their foot or forget to cover the ball or to turn their ankle.
- Demonstrate the exercise so that the players watch from behind.
- Start practicing slowly and then increase speed.
- If the trick is performed with the left foot, the player turns to the right. The opposite with the right foot.

Field size:
A box between 5-30 m depending upon group size. An alternative could also be the 18-yard box

Distance between the cones:
Depending upon group size 5-30 m.

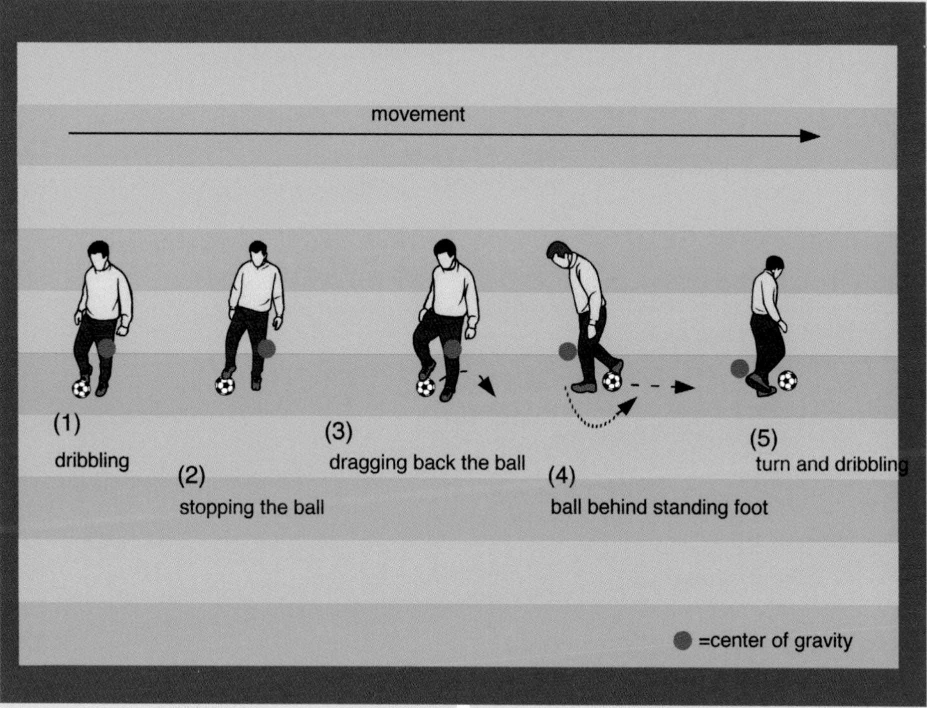

13 Sole of the Foot (Drag Back)

Training Target

- **Ball skill (Touch on the ball)**

Training Emphasis

- **Finesse on the ball**
- **Feinting/trick dribbling**
- **Fitness program**
- **Coordination**

Training Aspects

Skills involved:	Speed of movement with ball, Quick anticipation, Outside of the foot, Trapping into space, Dribbling, Quick decision-making, Quick processing, Inside of the foot, Combining technical skill with movement, Speed in change of direction
Age level:	6-8 years, 9- 12 years, 13-14 years, 15 years to Adult
Level of play:	Recreational
Type of training:	Individual training, Group training
Training structure:	Warm-up, Conclusion, Progression
Purpose:	Improve individual qualities
Total number of players:	2 or more players
Participating players:	Whole team
Training location:	Any
Spatial awareness:	Free space
Duration:	1-10 min
Physiology:	Soccer-specific endurance, Speed endurance, Power & Speed, Explosiveness training

Organization:
One ball per player.

Implementation:
The players dribble with the ball, stop and drag the ball back with the sole of the foot behind their supporting foot, turn 180 degrees and dribble off in the opposite direction.

Note:

- The standing leg should be next to the ball when dragging the ball back.
- The movement should not be too severe.
- Quick, fluid movements.

Field size:
free

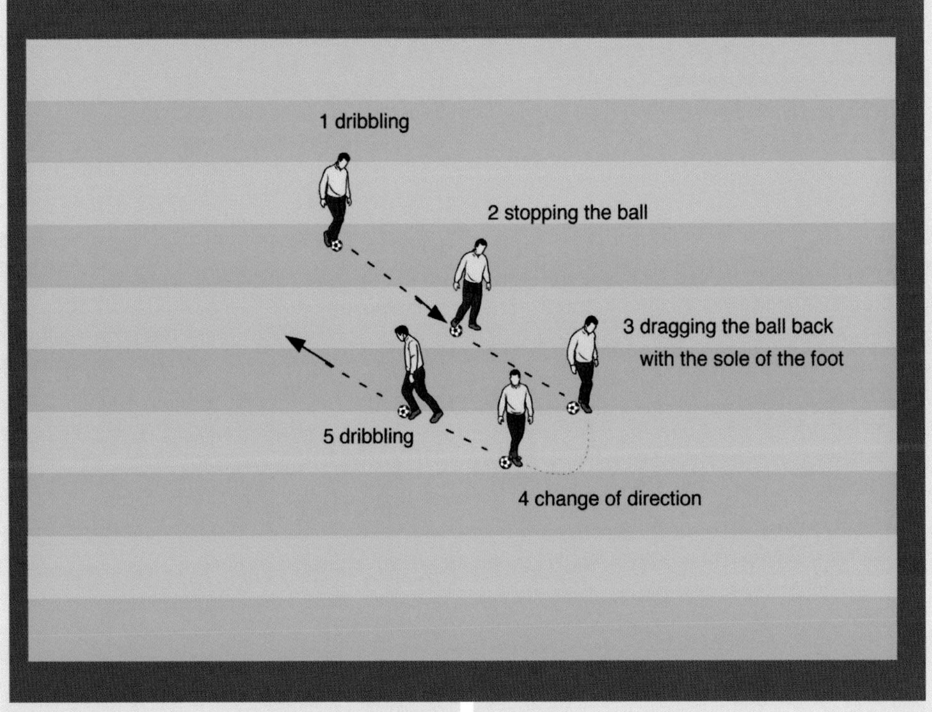

14 Fake Shot Trick + Flicking with the Instep

Training Target

- Ball skill (Touch on the ball)

Training Emphasis

- Dribbling control
- Finesse on the ball
- Feinting/trick dribbling
- Fitness program
- Coordination

Training Aspects

Skills involved:	Speed of movement with ball, Offensive play, Quick anticipation, Outside of the foot, Control, Trapping into space, Dribbling, Quick decision-making, Quick processing, Inside of the foot, Variable intervals, Bodyfake, Combining technical skill with movement, Quickness of reaction, Speed in change of direction, Laces
Age level:	Any age
Level of play:	Recreational
Type of training:	Individual training, Group training, Team training
Training structure:	Warm-up, Conclusion, Progression, Main point/Emphasis
Purpose:	Attack behavior, Improve individual qualities
Total number of players:	2 or more players
Participating players:	Whole team
Training location:	Any
Spatial awareness:	Free space
Duration:	5-10 min
Physiology:	Soccer-specific endurance, Speed endurance, Power & Speed

Organization:
The trick can be practiced in a coned-in area or anywhere where the player has some space. One ball per player.

Implementation:
The player swings his foot over the ball as if he were shooting. Then he flicks the ball sideways in the same movement with his instep or outstep, past his opponent at an angle of 90 degrees.

Note:

- The fake shot trick is a full body movement. As a result, the player should make sure that he keeps his body upright as long as possible, until the last second before he flicks the ball to the side.
- The players should put in a short sprint after the trick.
- The player's supporting foot should be in front of the ball.

Field size:
free

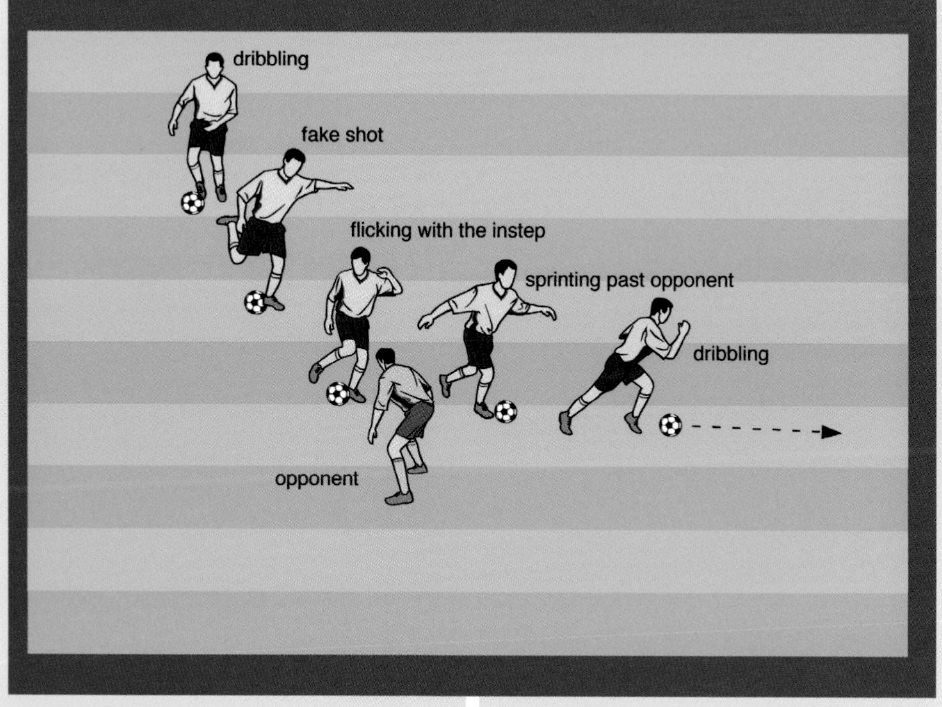

15 Fake Shot Trick + Dragging the Ball Back Behind the Supporting Foot

Training Target
- Ball skill (Touch on the ball)

Training Emphasis
- Finesse on the ball
- Feinting/trick dribbling
- Fitness program
- Coordination

Training Aspects

Skills involved:	Speed of movement with ball, Offensive play, Quick anticipation, Outside of the foot, Control, Trapping into space, Dribbling, Quick decision-making, Quick processing, Inside of the foot, Bodyfake, Combining skill with movement, Quickness of reaction, Speed in change of direction
Age level:	Any age
Level of play:	Recreational
Type of training:	Individual training, Group training
Training structure:	Warm-up, Conclusion, Progression
Purpose:	Attack behavior, Improve individual qualities
Total number of players:	2 or more players
Participating players:	Whole team
Training location:	Any
Spatial awareness:	Free space
Duration:	1-10 min
Physiology:	Soccer-specific endurance, Speed endurance, Power & Speed

Organization:
The trick can be practiced in a coned-in area or anywhere where the player has some space. One ball per player.

Implementation:
The player starts by dribbling, then dummies a shot with his right foot. His left supporting foot should be in front of the ball and then he drags the ball back behind his standing leg with his right instep, to the left. The player turns 90 degrees to the left and dribbles with his left outstep, past his opponent.

Note:
- The fake shot trick is a full body movement. As a result, the player should make sure that he keeps his body upright as long as possible, until the last second before he drags the ball back between his legs.

Field size:
free

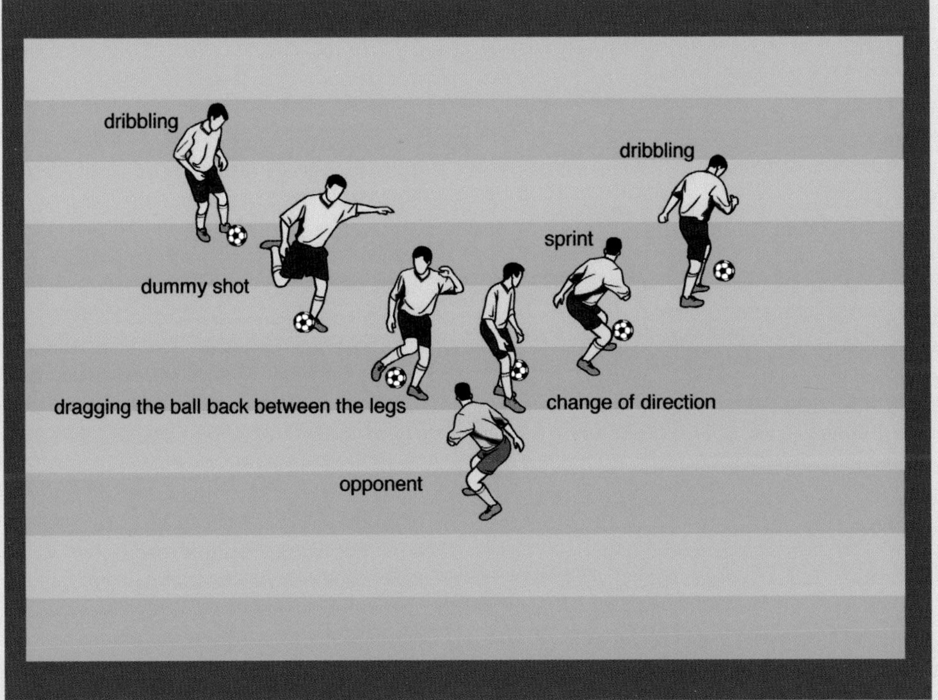

16 Ronaldo Trick I

Training Target

- Ball skill (Touch on the ball)

Training Emphasis

- Dribbling control
- Finesse on the ball
- Feinting/trick dribbling
- Fitness program
- Coordination

Training Aspects

Skills involved:	Speed of movement with ball, Quick anticipation, Outside of the foot, Control, Trapping into space, Dribbling, Quick decision-making, Quick processing, Inside of the foot, Bodyfake, Combining technical skill with movement, Quickness of reaction, Speed in change of direction
Age level:	Any age
Level of play:	Recreational
Type of training:	Individual training, Group training
Training structure:	Warm-up, Conclusion, Progression
Purpose:	Attack behavior, Improve individual qualities
Total number of players:	2 or more players
Participating players:	Whole team
Training location:	Any
Spatial awareness:	Free space
Duration:	1-10 min
Physiology:	Soccer-specific endurance, Power & Speed

Organization:
One ball per player.

Implementation:
The player starts by dribbling before knocking the ball to the left with his right instep/sole of the foot while moving his right foot over the ball from left to right. He then drags his left foot over the ball and knocks the ball with the outside of his left foot to the left and dribbles past his opponent.

Note:

- The Ronaldo trick is a full body movement. As a result, the player should make sure that he leans his body in the opposite direction (right) from the movement of the ball (left).
- The player should attempt to distract his opponent with his upper body movement, and to try to convince his opponent to make the same movement. The player with the ball can gain time with this movement.
- The players should stroke the ball with their instep/sole of their foot.
- The upper body should be slightly leaning forward.
- The players should complete this trick on the balls of their feet.
- At the start of the trick the players should keep their movements (upper body swing and step over) short and quick and not make long, slow movements.
- The exercise should be started slowly without any obstacles or opponents. As the player becomes more confident, the

speed can be increased and an obstacle (cone) introduced. Finally, the trick should be completed with an opponent.

- Short, quick movements.
- The player should not only look down at the ball, he should vary his view between player and ball.
- After the trick, the player should move the ball slightly to the left with the outside of the cleat.
- Short, quick sprint.

Field size:
free

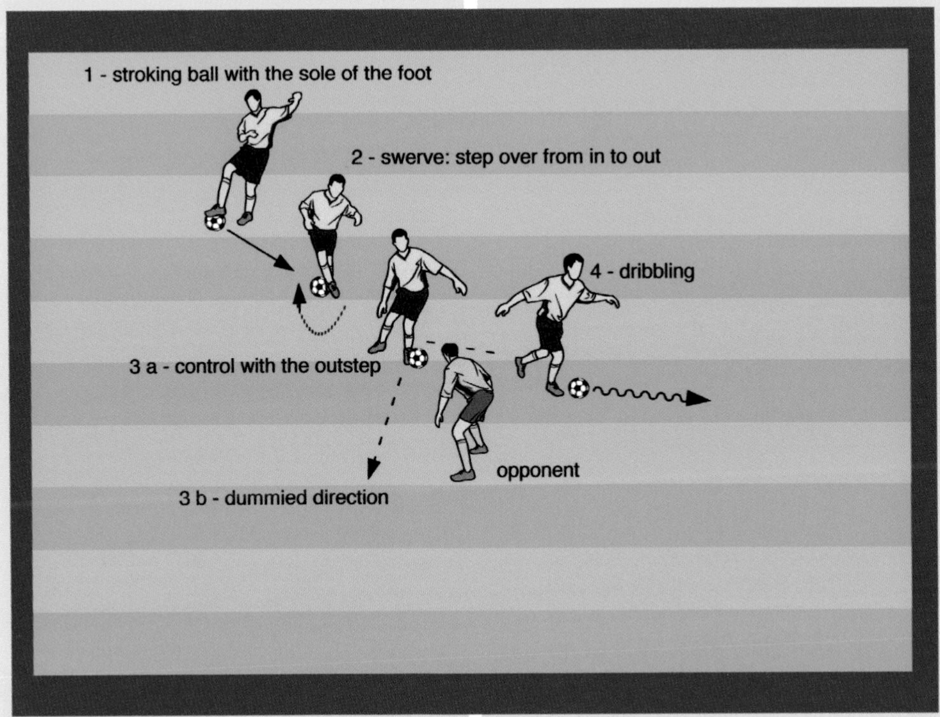

17 Ronaldo Trick II

Training Target
- **Ball skill (Touch on the ball)**

Training Emphasis
- **Dribbling control**
- **Finesse on the ball**
- **Feinting/trick dribbling**
- **Fitness program**
- **Coordination**

Training Aspects

Skills involved:	**Speed of movement with ball, Quick anticipation, Outside of the foot, Control, Trapping into space, Dribbling, Quick decision-making, Quick processing, Inside of the foot, Bodyfake, Combining technical skill with movement,, Quickness of reaction, Speed in change of direction**
Age level:	**Any age**
Level of play:	**Recreational**
Type of training:	**Individual training, Group training**
Training structure:	**Warm-up, Conclusion, Progression**
Purpose:	**Attack behavior, Improve individual qualities**
Total number of players:	**2 or more players**
Participating players:	**Whole team**
Training location:	**Any**
Spatial awareness:	**Free space**
Duration:	**1-10 min**
Physiology:	**Soccer-specific endurance, Power & Speed**

Organization:
One ball per player.

Implementation:
The player starts dribbling, then passes the ball with the sole of the right foot/instep to the left and moves the left foot from the right, in, over the ball. (Fake shot trick). He then passes the ball, with the outside of the left cleat, to the left and dribbles past his opponent.

Note:
- The players should stroke the ball with their instep/sole of their foot.
- The upper body should be slightly leaning forwards.
- The players should complete this trick on the balls of their feet.
- The fake shot trick is a full body movement. As a result, the player should make sure that he moves his body away from the ball until the last minute before touching the ball. He moves his shooting foot over the ball, quickly touches his foot down directly behind the ball in order to flick the ball to the side with his outstep. When he completes this trick with his right foot, he steps over the ball from right to left and then moves away with the ball with his right outstep. At the start of the trick the players should keep their movements (upper body swing and step over) short and quick and not make long, slow movements.
- The exercise should be started slowly without any obstacles or opponents. As the player becomes more confident, the

speed can be increased and an obstacle (cone) introduced. Finally the trick should be completed with an opponent.

- Short, quick movements.
- The player should not only look down at the ball. He should vary his view between player and ball.
- After the trick the player should move the ball slightly to the left with the outside of the cleat.
- Short, quick sprint.

Field size:
free

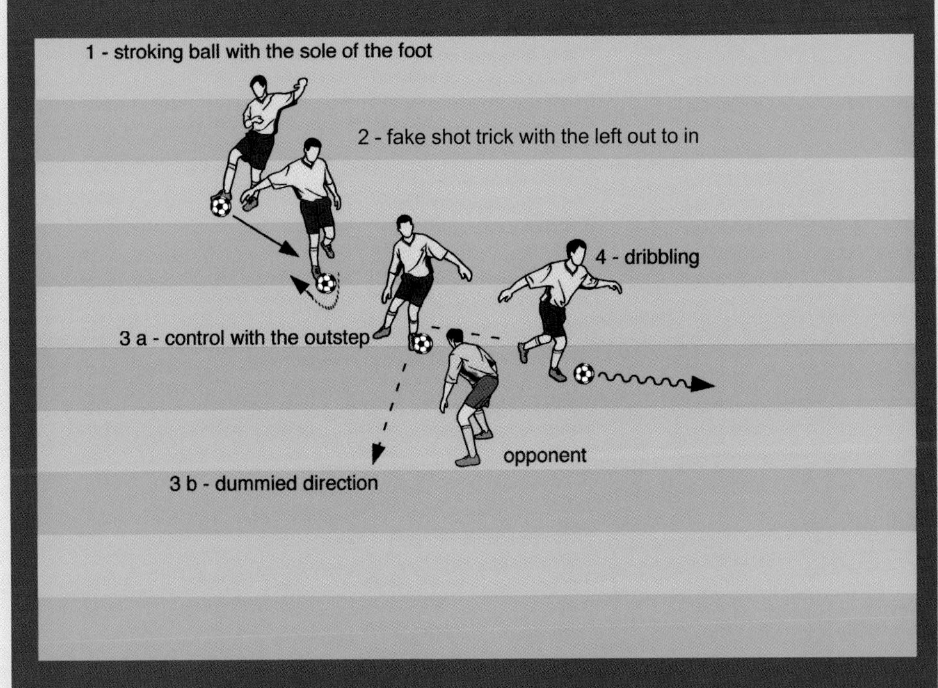

18 360-Degree Turn

Training Target

- Ball skill (Touch on the ball)

Training Emphasis

- Dribbling control
- Finesse on the ball
- Feinting/trick dribbling
- Fitness program
- Coordination

Training Aspects

Skills involved:	Leaping strength, Speed of movement with ball, Quick anticipation, Outside of the foot, Control, Trapping into space, Flexibility, Dribbling, Quick decision-making, Quick processing, Inside of the foot, Bodyfake, Combining technical skill with movement, Quickness of reaction, Speed in change of direction, Laces
Age level:	Any age
Level of play:	Recreational
Type of training:	Individual training, Group training
Training structure:	Warm-up, Conclusion, Progression
Purpose:	Attack behavior, Improve individual qualities
Total number of players:	2 or more players
Participating players:	Whole team
Training location:	Any
Spatial awareness:	Free space
Duration:	1-10 min
Physiology:	Soccer-specific endurance, Speed endurance, Power & Speed

Organization:
The players find space within the playing area and each has a ball.

Implementation:
The player starts dribbling. If he dribbles with his right foot, he lifts his leg up so that his knee makes a 90 degree angle. He then touches the ball with his the sole of his right foot, turns 180 degrees to the left, over his left shoulder, and places his left foot down next to the ball (with his back to his opponent). He then drags the ball back with the sole of his left foot (with his left leg bent 90 degrees as before) and turns a further 180 degrees. The player has now returned to his starting position. During this movement, the player should place his left leg down next to the ball and move off to the right, using the outside of his right foot.

Note:
- Turn into the opponent, sprint away off to the side.
- At first practice slowly.
- To turn correctly, the player can place his hand on the shoulder over which he would like to turn.
- Quick, fluid movements.

Field size:
free

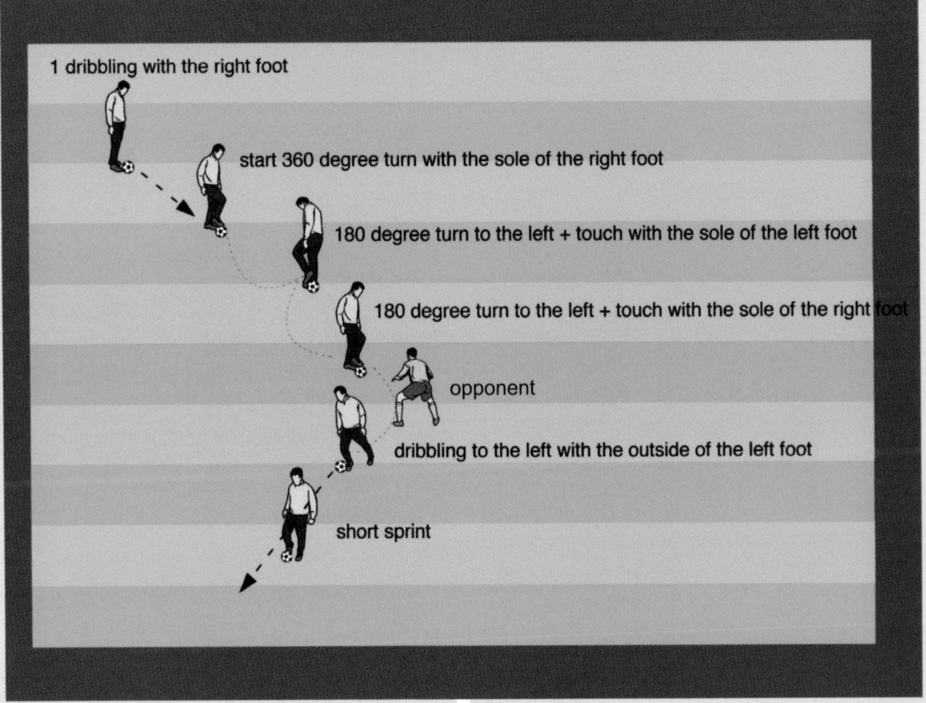

20 Okocha Trick

Training Target
- **Ball skill (Touch on the ball)**

Training Emphasis
- **Finesse on the ball**
- **Feinting/trick dribbling**
- **Coordination**

Training Aspects

Skills involved:	Speed of movement with ball, Trapping into space, Combining technical skill with movement
Age level:	13-14 years, 15 years to Adult
Level of play:	Advanced, Professional
Type of training:	Individual training, Group training
Training structure:	Warm-up, Conclusion, Progression
Purpose:	Improve individual qualities
Total number of players:	2 or more players
Participating players:	Whole team
Training location:	Any
Spatial awareness:	Free space
Duration:	5-10 min
Physiology:	Soccer-specific endurance

Organization:
One ball per player.

Implementation:
The player dribbles with the ball. During the dribble, the player traps the ball between his front and back feet. The feet should be so placed, that the heel of the player's front foot is backed into the ball with the instep of the back foot behind the ball. At the moment of contact between both feet, the back foot lightly presses the ball against the heel of the front foot. The front foot should now be quickly flicked upwards so that the ball is thrown upwards into the air behind the player's body. The flick has to be hard enough to propel the ball over the player's head in front of him. The player can now control the ball and continue with the dribble. After a few meters the player should attempt the Okocha trick again.

Note:
- Keep the pace up during the trick.
- The upper body should be turned while the ball is flicked over the player's head so that the player can look over his shoulder, back towards the ball.
- The player should make a short sprint after the trick (2-3 meters).
- After the player has practiced without an opponent, he should attempt the trick with a cone and then against a passive opponent and then against an active opponent.
- When practicing against an opponent, the ball should be flicked over the head of the opponent.
- The ball must be brought under control immediately after the trick in order for the player to be able to free himself from his opponent.

Field size:
free

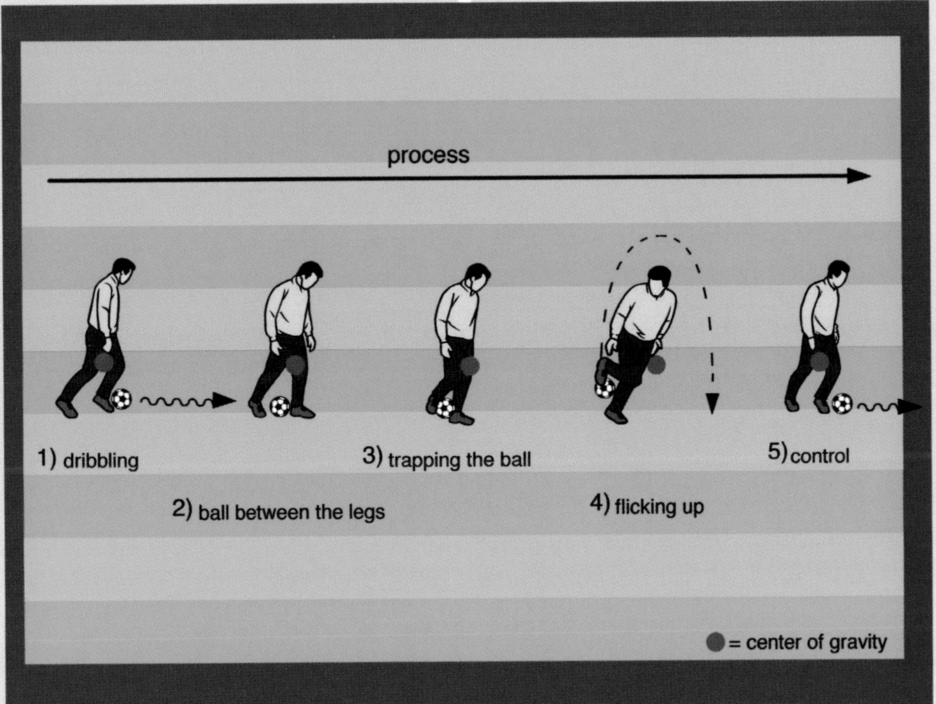

21 Locomotive

Training Target
- Ball skill (Touch on the ball)

Training Emphasis
- Finesse on the ball
- Feinting/trick dribbling
- Coordination

Training Aspects	
Skills involved:	Speed of movement with ball, Quick anticipation, Outside of the foot, Control, Trapping into space, Dribbling, Quick decision-making, Quick processing, Combining technical skill with movement, Quickness of reaction, Laces, Quick understanding of danger
Age level:	Any age
Level of play:	Recreational
Type of training:	Individual training, Group training
Training structure:	Warm-up, Conclusion, Progression
Purpose:	Attack behavior, Improve individual qualities
Total number of players:	2 or more players
Participating players:	Whole team
Training location:	Any
Spatial awareness:	Free space
Duration:	1-10 min
Physiology:	Soccer-specific endurance, Training of elementary endurance II, Speed endurance, Power & Speed

Organization:
One ball per player.

Implementation:
The movement should copy the movement of an old locomotive. The foot goes over the ball and the player fakes backheeling the ball. The player reduces speed. Instead of backheeling the ball, the player flicks the ball with the laces in the original direction and rapidly increases tempo (sprint). The player should attempt to outwit his opponent through the change of speed and body swerve.

Note:
- Practice slowly at first and then increase speed.
- Quick, fluid movements with the leg/foot.
- Bend leg 90 degrees.

Field size:
free

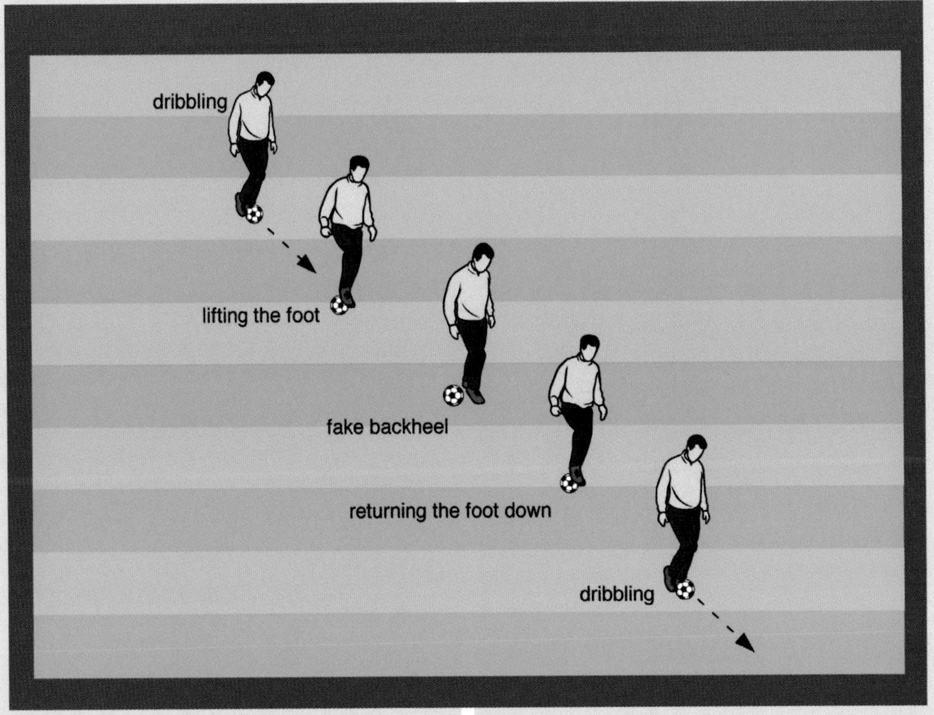

Training Target
- **Ball skill (Touch on the ball)**

Training Emphasis
- **Dribbling control**
- **Finesse on the ball**
- **Feinting/trick dribbling**
- **Coordination**

Training Aspects

Skills involved:	Speed of movement with ball, Quick anticipation, Outside of the foot, Control, Trapping into space, Speed of movement off the ball, Dribbling, Quick decision-making, Quick processing, Inside of the foot, Variable intervals, Bodyfake, Combining technical skill with movement, Running technique with/without ball, Quickness of reaction, Speed in change of direction, Laces, Quick understanding of danger
Age level:	Any age
Level of play:	Beginner, Recreational, Advanced, Professional
Type of training:	Team training
Training structure:	Warm-up, Progression
Purpose:	Individual training, Improve individual qualities
Total number of players:	6 or more players
Participating players:	Whole team
Training location:	Any
Spatial awareness:	Limited playing field
Duration:	10-30 min
Physiology:	Soccer-specific endurance, Strength endurance, Speed endurance, Power & Speed

Organization:
A box. One ball per player.

Implementation:
To help the players to learn a new move or skill it is advisable to use the following steps:

1. Place the group in front of the coach.
2. Slowly explain and demonstrate the movement; first in front of the group and then with the group behind the coach. (Easier for the child to imitate.)
3. Get the children to imitate the movement while standing still.
4. Get the children to slowly imitate the action.
5. Gradually increase the speed until you reach the demonstration speed.

Swerves, dodges and dribbling techniques

Fundamentally, tricks are body movements. As a result, the movement of the upper body is essential. Exercises should always be trained with both feet. The players should have lots of touches on the ball, always be in control of the ball, and dribble with the ball close to their body, so that their opponent cannot easily get to the ball.

Note:
The aim is to out-maneuver the opponent and to leave him behind, consequently it is important to increase speed after the trick has been completed (a short sprint for about 2m). Feel free to start slowly and then increase your speed during the trick. To commit the movement correctly to muscle memory, it is essential that the coach permanently corrects, demonstrates and communicates with the player. It is essential with dribbling techniques and tricks that the player repeats the movement as often as possible and has a high number of touches on the ball.

Tricks:
Individual tricks can be assigned a number. Trick "X" would be, e.g., trick number 1, Trick "Y" would be trick 2 etc. The coach calls out the different numbers and the players have to think before completing the corresponding trick. This improves concentration, communication (the players should call out tricks themselves) and, last but not least, game intelligence. The tricks can also be combined together with the use of double figures, e.g. 12 (first trick 1, then trick 2), 21 (first 2 then 1), 11 (2x trick 1), 323 (first trick 3, then 2, then 3 again), etc.

Dribbling techniques:
An order can also be assigned to dribbling techniques. It is advisable to assign letters to this skill though, so that the players can later combine the dribbling skills with tricks.

Example:
a) Change of direction while dribbling with the right instep (max. 3 touches).
b) ...with the left instep.
c) ...with the right outstep.
d) ...with the left outstep.

This gives us the following combinations of tricks:

1a) Completion of trick 1 with a subsequent change of direction with a flick of the right instep
12c) Completion trick 1, completion trick 2 with a subsequent change of direction with a flick of the right outstep etc.

- Juggling -The ball should not spin (the words on the ball should always be visible) when juggling. => It is therefore advisable to stretch out the foot. The toes should not be turned upwards towards the upper body and the sole of the foot should be parallel to the ground. Use both feet! (why? – because they are both the same size!) Give targets. When a target has been reached, set new targets: (When 10 have been achieved, move onto 12 etc.).

If the level of the group is not high, introducing the juggling skills can take the following shape:

1. The ball can be held in the hands at the start. The sequence then runs as follows: drop the ball from the hands onto the right foot —> Catch the ball. Drop the ball onto the left foot —> Catch the ball, etc.

2. Without hands. The ball is only allowed to bounce once. Sequence: Right foot —› one bounce —› left foot —› one bounce —› right foot, etc.
3. Without bouncing.
4. Further steps: (a) left/right foot, left/right knee (b) Foot/head/knee (c) Foot/knee/shoulder/head/shoulder/knee/foot

Note:

- Requires high levels of concentration.
- Demand precision and high speed.
- Demonstrate each exercise in front of the group. Then let the players imitate your demonstration. Then correct and give detailed explanations to each movement.
- It is important that the explanation doesn't become information overload.
- The player should learn to observe and imitate what he has observed. Similar to in a game situation. In a game, the coach can't instruct the player what to do and how to react in every situation.
- Permanently correct mistakes, this ensures that the player doesn't develop any wrong habits.
- The coach should assemble the group in front of him when explaining a technique and not forget to demonstrate the skill with his back to the players as well.
- The coach should find the right mix of words in his explanation. A combination of clarity and empathy.
- The coach can imitate stressful situations with talented groups by verbally increasing the pressure on the players.

Training Target
- Ball skill (Touch on the ball)

Training Emphasis
- Finesse on the ball
- Feinting/trick dribbling

Training Aspects

Skills involved:	Speed of movement with ball, Quick anticipation, Controlling the ball, One touch passes, Quick decision-making, Quick processing, Inside of the foot, Inside of the foot passing, Inside of the laces passing, Bodyfake, Combining technical skill with movement, Short passing, Quickness of reaction, Quick understanding of danger
Age level:	6-8 years, 9-12 years, 13-14 years, 15 years to Adult
Level of play:	Advanced
Type of training:	Training in pairs
Training structure:	Warm-up, Progression
Purpose:	Improve individual qualities
Total number of players:	2 or more players
Participating players:	Whole team
Training location:	Any
Spatial awareness:	Limited playing field
Duration:	10-15 min
Physiology:	Soccer-specific endurance, Speed endurance, Power & Speed

Organization:
Two players start at opposite cones, 1 ball.

Implementation:
The player with ball passes the ball to the opposing player. When the player in possession passes, the player awaiting the pass makes a short dummy run towards the ball so that he receives the ball approx. level with the cone. The player takes the ball with his right foot and flicks the ball behind his standing leg to his left foot. His next touch is with his left foot and should move the ball into the right position to complete a stepover. The player starts the stepover with his right foot and then passes back to the opposing player with his left foot. The exercise then continuously follows this pattern.The direction of the drill should be changed every 3-5 minutes so that the control and stepover are completed with the left foot and the pass with the right foot.

Note:
- The pass must be hit on the ground, be precise and be struck with the correct foot.
- The dummy movement should take place at the same time as the player passes.
- The dummy movement should be in a sideways direction.
- The control and the flick onto the other foot, behind the standing leg, should be done with the instep. This should all be done in one, fluid movement. The player's foot should be moved towards the oncoming ball. The player should move his foot away from the ball, slightly slower

than the pace of the ball, just before the ball arrives at his foot. The ball can now be controlled slowly and led with the instep.

- Because of the complexity of the skill, the passes should not be hit too hard for groups with a lower skill level (e.g. beginners or children).
- Make sure that the stepover after the backheel is completed correctly (the stepover is a body trick, that means that the player should deliberately swerve his body sideways to influence the movement of his imaginary opponent.
- It should be the aim to complete this combination of skills, coordination and concentration techniques as quickly as possible.

Field size:
6 x 15 m

Distance between the cones:
15 m

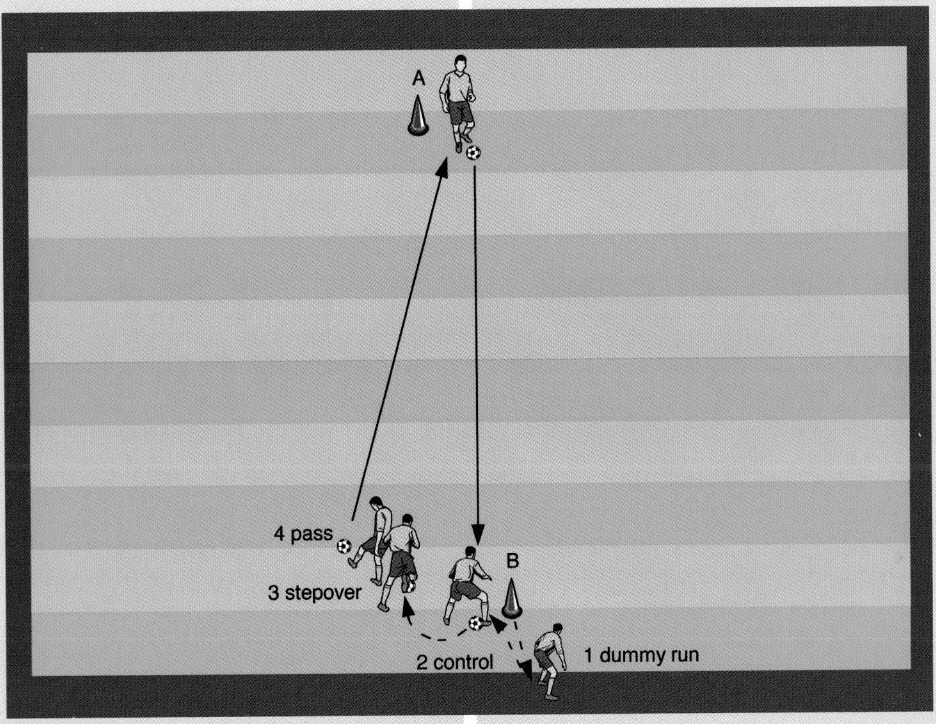

Training Target

- Ball skill (Touch on the ball)

Training Emphasis

- Trapping
- Finesse on the ball
- Feinting/trick dribbling
- Fitness program

Training Aspects

Skills involved:	Speed of movement with ball, Quick anticipation, Outside of the foot, Controlling the ball, One touch passes, Dribbling, Quick decision-making, Inside of the foot passing, Bodyfake, Combining technical skill with movement
Age level:	9 - 12 years, 13 - 14 years, 15 years to Adult
Level of play:	Advanced
Type of training:	Group training
Training structure:	Warm-up, Progression
Purpose:	Attack behavior
Total number of players:	Improve individual qualities
Participating players:	Whole team
Training location:	any
Spatial awareness:	Limited playing field
Duration:	5-10 min
Physiology:	Soccer-specific endurance, Explosiveness, Power & Speed

Organization:
Two player start at opposing cones. One ball.

Implementation:
Player A passes precisely on the ground to player B. When the player in possession passes, the player awaiting the pass makes a short run towards the ball. Player B should control the ball with the outside of the boot. Player B then pretends to shoot before passing back to player A who then does the same. The exercise then continuously follows this pattern.

Note:
- The pass must be precise.
- The pass should be hit hard.
- The player receiving the ball should focus on his timing. He should move when the player in possession begins to strike the ball.
- One touch.
- The faked shot is a body movement. The players should try to make their movement look like a shot until the last possible moment when they actually start the intended ball trick. The player does this by swinging the shooting foot towards the ball and stabbing it sharply into the ground just behind the ball before flicking the ball to the side with his outstep. If the player completes the trick with his right foot, then he should swing his foot from right to left, over the ball before flicking the ball away with his right outstep.

- The player should complete a short sprint (approx. 2 m) after the trick and before passing.
- The distances would always be held the same, i.e. the players not in possession wait next to their cone.
- Train both feet.

Field size:
8 x 25 m

Distance between the cones:
ca. 25 m

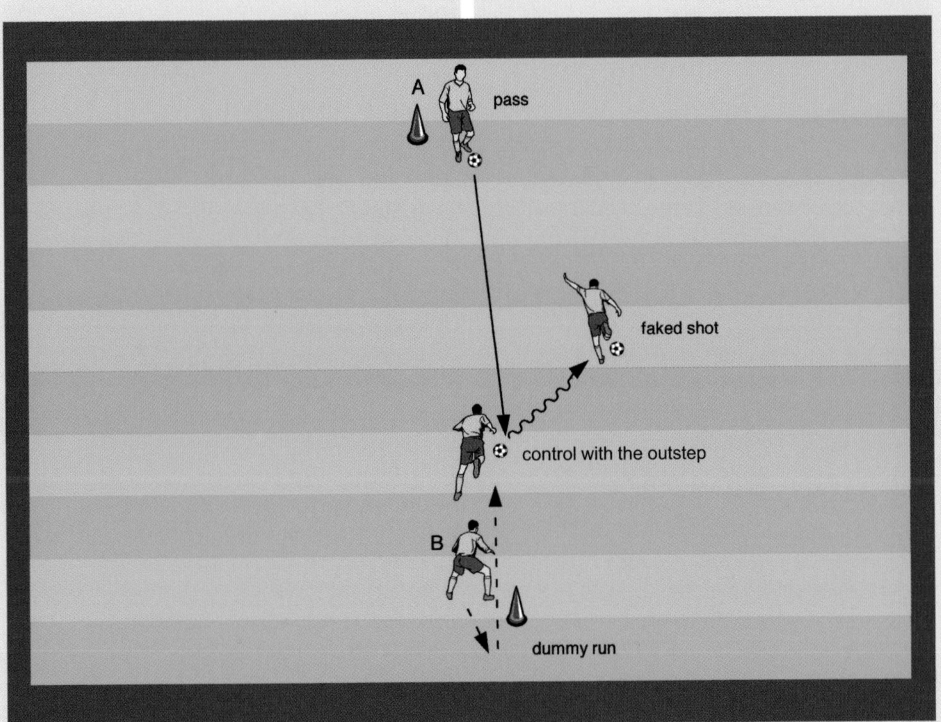

Training Target
- **Ball skill (Touch on the ball)**

Training Emphasis
- **Finesse on the ball**

Training Aspects

Skills involved:	**Speed of movement with ball, Quick anticipation, Outside of the foot, Controlling the ball, Quick decision-making, Combining technical skill with movement, Speed in change of direction**
Age level:	**9-12 years, 13-14 years, 15 years to Adult**
Level of play:	**Advanced**
Type of training:	**Individual training, Group training**
Training structure:	**Warm-up, Progression**
Purpose:	**Attack behavior, Improve individual qualities**
Total number of players:	**1-2 players, 2 or more players**
Participating players:	**Whole team**
Training location:	**Any**
Spatial awareness:	**Limited playing field**
Duration:	**5-10 min**
Physiology:	**Soccer-specific endurance, Power & Speed**

Organization:
Set up one cone per player on the field. The cones should be laid out so that each player has enough space to practice without being disturbed by the other players. One ball per player.

Implementation:
The players juggle the ball. After a certain number of touches the players should then play the ball into the air and then control the ball again with the in- or outstep as it comes down. After controlling the ball, the players should complete a short sprint (approx. 2 m). The sequence then starts again from the start. Variation 1: The ball can also be controlled forwards with the sole of the players' foot instead of sideways.

Note:
- The player can decide whether he hits the ball straight up into the air or slightly forwards. The player should try to control the ball out of the air while standing still and while in movement.
- The ball must be brought under control at the second when the ball touches the floor. If the skill is completed properly then the ball won't bounce away from the player and can be controlled with his next touch.
- In order to stop the ball from bouncing away and to ensure fluid and quick control, the players have to have good timing and use the right technique and ball control.
- The ball should not bounce further away from the player than 50 cm - 1 m.
- Control should always be coached with both feet.

- When controlling the ball with the sole of the foot, the players' upper body should remain upright and the players' toes should be tensed.

Field size:
10 x 10 m

Distance between the cones:
10 m in both directions.

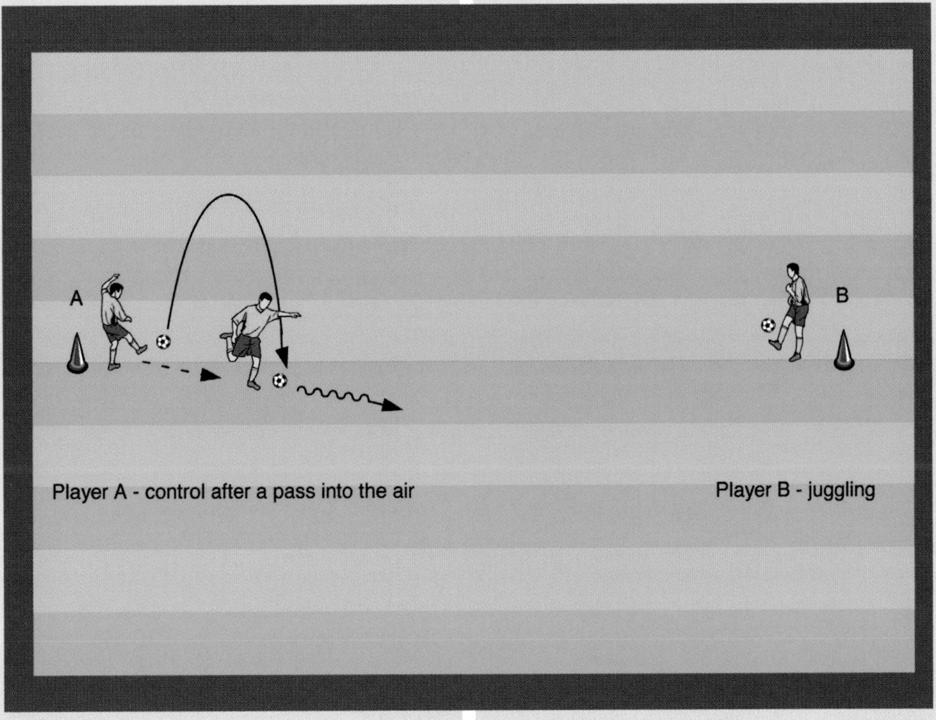

Training Target
- **Ball skill (Touch on the ball)**

Training Emphasis
- **Finesse on the ball**
- **Fitness program**

Training Aspects

Skills involved:	**Speed of movement with ball, Quick anticipation, Controlling the ball, Dribbling, Combining technical skill with movement, Laces**
Age level:	**9-12 years, 13-14 years, 15 years to Adult**
Level of play:	**Advanced**
Type of training:	**Individual training, Group training**
Training structure:	**Warm-up, Progression**
Purpose:	**Improve individual qualities**
Total number of players:	**1-2 players, 2 or more players**
Participating players:	**Whole team**
Training location:	**Any**
Spatial awareness:	**Limited playing field**
Duration:	**5-10 min**
Physiology:	**Soccer-specific endurance, Power & Speed, Explosiveness training**

Organization:
Set up one cone
per player on the field. The cones should be laid out so that each player has enough space to practice without being disturbed by the other players. One ball per player.

Implementation:
The players juggle the ball. After a certain number of touches the players should then play the ball into the air and then control the ball again with their laces so that the ball rolls through the players' legs. After controlling the ball with their first touch, the players should turn 180 degrees and then perform a short sprint (approx. 2 m). The sequence then starts again.

Note:
- The player can decide whether he hits the ball straight up into the air or slightly forwards. The player should try to control the ball out of the air while standing still and while in movement.
- It is important that the ball is brought under control with the player's first touch.
- The ball must be brought under control the second when the ball touches the floor. If the skill is completed properly then the ball won't bounce away from the player and can be controlled with his next touch.
- In order to stop the ball from bouncing away and to ensure fluid and quick control, the players have to have good timing and use the right technique and ball control.
- The ball should not bounce further away from the player than 50 cm-1 m.
- Control should always be coached with both feet.

Field size:
10 x 10 m

Distance between the cones:
Approx. 10 m on both sides

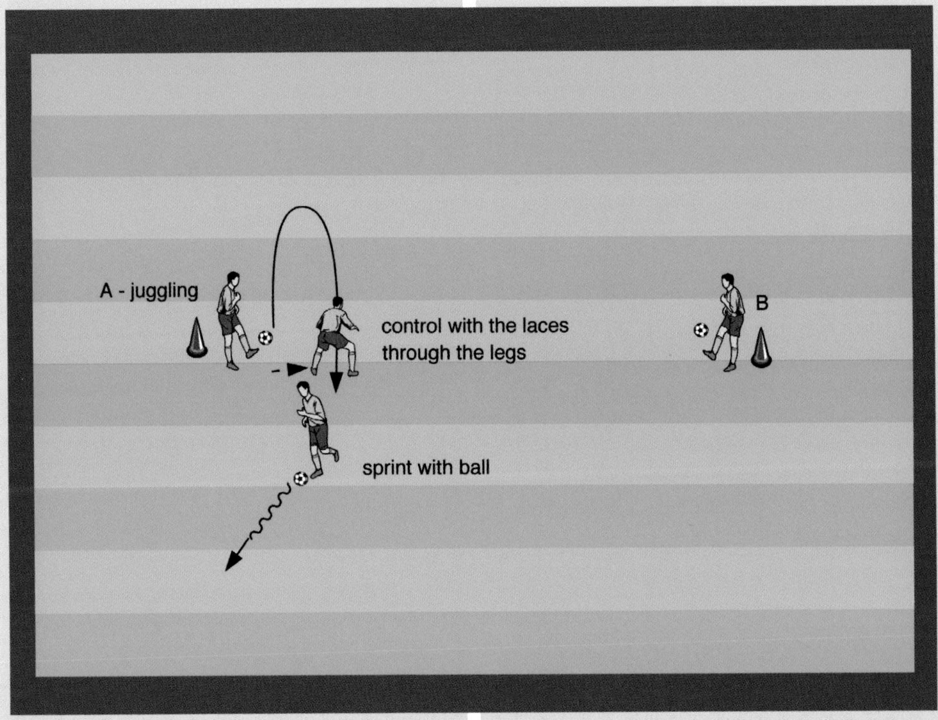

27 Touch V

Training Target
- **Ball skill (Touch on the ball)**

Training Emphasis
- **Finesse on the ball**

Training Aspects

Skills involved:	Control, Combining technical skill with movement, Volley
Age level:	13-14 years, 15 years to Adult
Level of play:	Advanced, Professional
Type of training:	Training in pairs
Training structure:	Warm-up, Conclusion, Progression
Purpose:	Training for fun, Improve individual qualities
Total number of players:	2 or more players
Participating players:	Whole team
Training location:	Any
Spatial awareness:	Limited playing field
Duration:	5-10 min

Organization:
Set up two cones opposite one another. One player starts at each cone with a ball.

Implementation:
The player in possession juggles the ball and then volleys the ball to their partner (after a call from the coach). The partner continues to juggle the ball, ensuring that it doesn't touch the ground before volleying the ball back to the first player.

Alternative:
- The exercise can also be organized as a game. Each mistake (ball touches the ground, inaccurate pass) means a point to the other player.
- A box (approx. 5 x 5 meters) can also be setup for the players to complete the exercise. Alternatively each player can stand in their own box.

Note:
The ball can be controlled with the following techniques:

- with the instep
- with the outstep
- with the laces
- with the thigh
- with the chest
- with the head

Field size:
5 x 20 m

Distance between the cones:
20 m

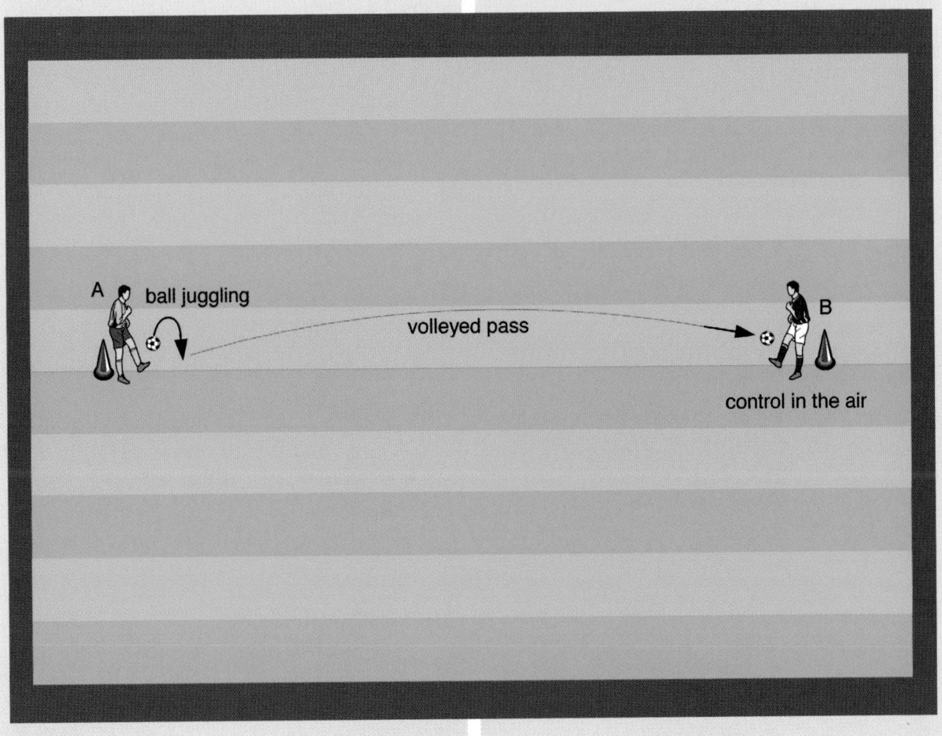

Training Target

- **Ball skill (Touch on the ball)**

Training Emphasis

- **Finesse on the ball**
- **Lifting the ball**
- **Ball control**

Training Aspects

Skills involved:	**Speed of movement with ball, Quick anticipation, Outside of the foot, Controlling the ball, Dribbling, Quick decisioning, Inside of the foot, Combining technical skill with movement, Running technique with/without ball**
Age level:	**9-12 years, 13-14 years, 15 years to Adult**
Level of play:	**Advanced**
Type of training:	**Individual training, Group training**
Training structure:	**Warm-up, Progression**
Purpose:	**Attack behavior, Improve individual qualities**
Total number of players:	**2 or more players**
Participating players:	**Whole team**
Training location:	**Any**
Spatial awareness:	**Limited playing field**
Duration:	**5-10 min**
Physiology:	**Soccer-specific endurance, Explosiveness, Power & Speed**

Organization:
Set up one cone per player on the field. The cones should be laid out so that each player has enough space to practice without being disturbed by the other players. One ball per player.

Implementation:
The players juggle the ball. After a certain number of touches the players should then play the ball into the air, spin 360 degrees and then control the ball with the instep or outstep. After controlling the ball with their first touch, the players should turn 180 degrees and then perform a short sprint (approx. 2 m). The sequence then starts again from the start.

Note:

- The player can decide whether he hits the ball straight up into the air or slightly forwards. The player should try to control the ball out of the air while standing still and while in movement.
- It is important that the ball is brought under control with the player's first touch.
- After the 360-degree turn, the ball has to be brought under control with the players' first touch. If the technique is correct, the ball shouldn't bounce away and should be able to be brought under control with the players first touch.
- The ball should not bounce further away than 50 cm-1 m.

Field size:
10 x 10 m

Distance between the cones:
10 m in all directions

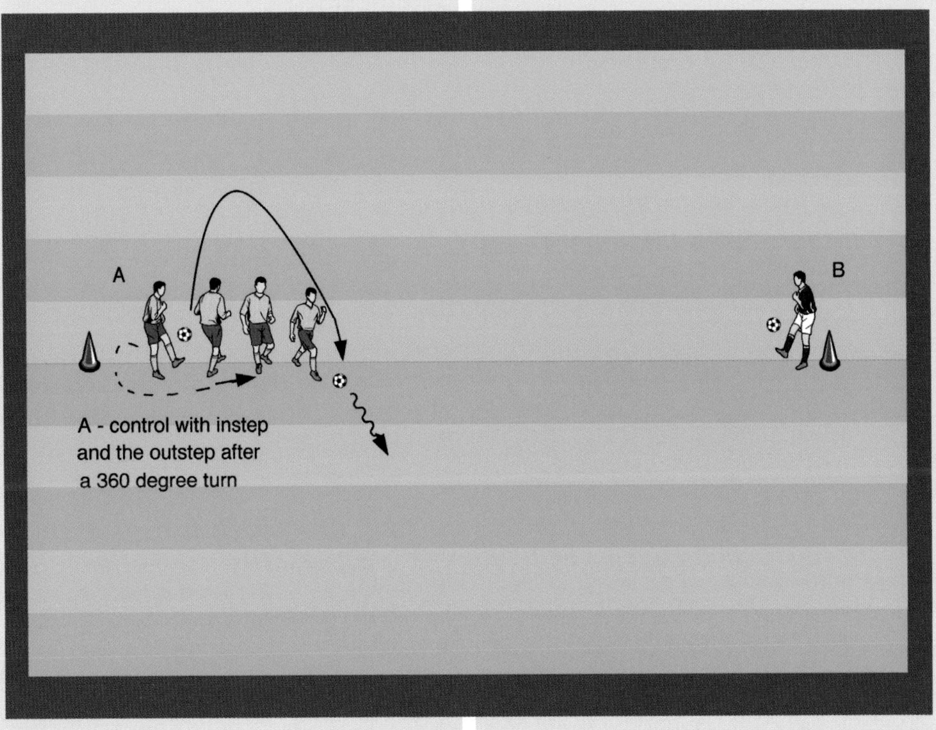

29 Touch VII

Training Target

- Ball skill (Touch on the ball)

Training Emphasis

- Finesse on the ball
- Lifting the ball
- Coordination

Training Aspects

Skills involved:	Control, Combining technical skill with movement
Age level:	9-12 years, 13-14 years, 15 years to Adult
Level of play:	Advanced
Type of training:	Individual training, Group training
Training structure:	Warm-up, Progression
Purpose:	Improve individual qualities
Total number of players:	2 or more players
Participating players:	Whole team
Training location:	Any
Spatial awareness:	Limited playing field
Duration:	5-10 min

Organization:
Set up one cone per player on the field. The cones should be laid out so that each player has enough space to practice without being disturbed by the other players. One ball per player.

Implementation:
The players hit the ball 50-100 cm into the air, let the ball drop and then play the ball with the right laces, let the ball drop, with the left laces, let the ball drop, with the left sole of the foot, let the ball drop, with the right sole of the foot, with the left laces etc. The sequence then starts again.

Note:

- The ball shouldn't be hit too high into the air.
- The upper body should be slightly leant forwards.
- Try to continuously increase the speed.
- Great practice for close control and touch.

Field size:
Depending upon number of players.
Calculation: 12 player = 10 x 15 m.

Distance between the cones:
Depending upon number of players.
Calculation: 12 player = 10 m wide; 15 m long.

30 Combined Juggling Techniques I

Training Target
- **Ball skill (Touch on the ball)**

Training Emphasis
- **Finesse on the ball**
- **Lifting the ball**
- **Juggling techniques**
- **Coordination**

Training Aspects

Skills involved:	Quick anticipation, Control, Quick decision-making, Inside of the foot, Combining technical skill with movement, Laces
Age level:	6-8 years, 9- 12 years, Any age
Level of play:	Beginner
Type of training:	Individual training, Group training
Training structure:	Warm-up, Conclusion, Progression
Purpose:	Improve individual qualities
Total number of players:	2 or more players
Participating players:	Whole team
Training location:	Any
Spatial awareness:	Free space
Duration:	1-10 min

Organization:
One ball per player.

Implementation:
The players drop the ball from their hands. When the ball rises the players then strike the ball alternately with their left and right foot. The sequence flows as follows: right foot - ground - left foot - ground, etc.

Note:
- The ball should be struck with the laces.
- Both feet should be used one after another.
- The upper body should be held upright, the players should keep their eyes on the ball.
- The standing leg should be slightly bent at the knee.
- The leg playing the ball should also be slightly bent at the knee. The knee should also be raised slightly so that the player's foot is free from the ground.
- The ball should be struck 20-30 cm above the ground.
- The arms remain at the side of the player's body and should be bent at the elbows (similar to the position when carrying buckets of water).
- The ball should be struck directly into the hands and too high into the air.
- The higher the player strikes the ball, the harder the exercise becomes.

Field size:
free

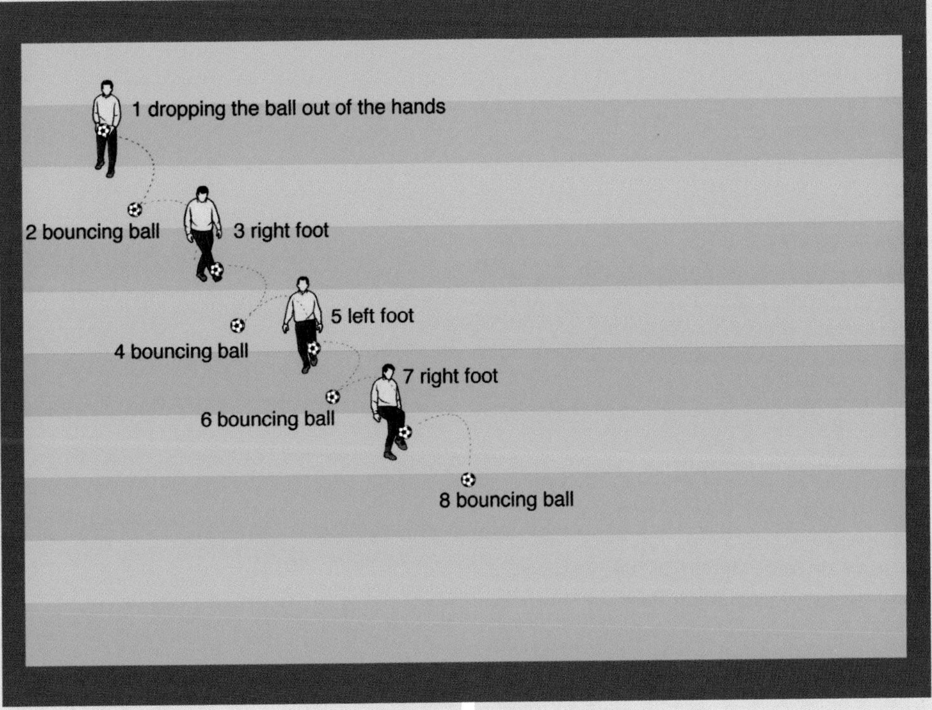

31 Combined Juggling Techniques II

Training Target

- Ball skill (Touch on the ball)

Training Emphasis

- Finesse on the ball
- Lifting the ball
- Juggling techniques
- Coordination

Training Aspects

Skills involved:	Speed of movement with ball, Quick anticipation, Control, Quick decision-making, Quick processing, Inside of the foot, Combining technical skill with movement, Volley, Laces, Quick understanding of danger
Age level:	6-8 years, 9- 12 years, 13- 14 years
Level of play:	Beginner
Type of training:	Individual training, Group training
Training structure:	Warm-up, Conclusion, Progression
Purpose:	Improve individual qualities
Total number of players:	2 or more players
Participating players:	Whole team
Training location:	Any
Spatial awareness:	Free space
Duration:	1-10 min

Organization:
One ball per player.

Implementation:
The players drop the ball from their hands. When the ball rises the players then knock the ball back into their hands without the ball touching the ground. The sequence flows as follows: right foot - catch - left foot - catch.

Note:
- The ball should be struck with the laces.
- Both feet should be used one after another.
- The upper body should be held upright, the players should keep their eyes on the ball.
- The standing leg should be slightly bent at the knee.
- The leg playing the ball should also be slightly bent at the knee. The knee should also be raised slightly so that the player's foot is free from the ground.
- The ball should be struck 20-30 cm above the ground.
- The arms remain at the side of the player's body and should be bent at the elbows (similar to the position when carrying buckets of water).
- The ball should be struck directly into the hands and not too high into the air.

Field size:
free

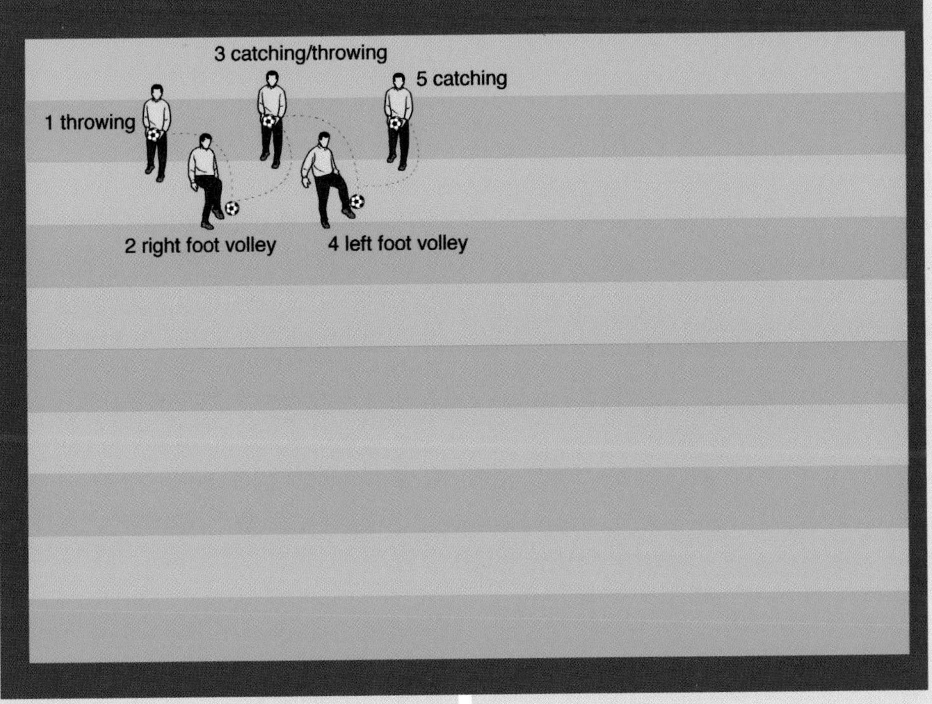

Training Target
- Ball skill (Touch on the ball)

Training Emphasis
- Finesse on the ball
- Lifting the ball
- Juggling techniques

Training Aspects

Skills involved:	Speed of movement with ball, Quick anticipation, Control, Quick processing, Combining technical skill with movement, Laces
Age level:	6-8 years, 9-12 years
Level of play:	Beginner
Type of training:	Type of training, Individual training
Training structure:	Warm-up, Conclusion, Progression
Purpose:	Improve individual qualities
Total number of players:	2 or more players
Participating players:	Whole team
Training location:	Any
Spatial awareness:	Free space
Duration:	1-10 min

Organization:
One ball per player

Implementation:
The players drop the ball from their hands onto the ground. When the ball rises, the players then complete a left/right combination (without the ball touching the ground between touches), let the ball drop to the ground again and then complete a right/left combination.

Note:
- The ball should be struck with the laces.
- Both feet should be used one after another.
- The upper body should be held upright, the players should keep their eyes on the ball.
- The standing leg should be slightly bent at the knee.
- The leg playing the ball should also be slightly bent at the knee. The knee should also be raised slightly so that the player's foot is free from the ground.
- The ball should be struck 20-30 cm above the ground.
- The arms remain at the side of the player's body and should be bent at the elbows (similar to the position when carrying buckets of water).
- The ball should not be struck too high into the air.

Field size:
free

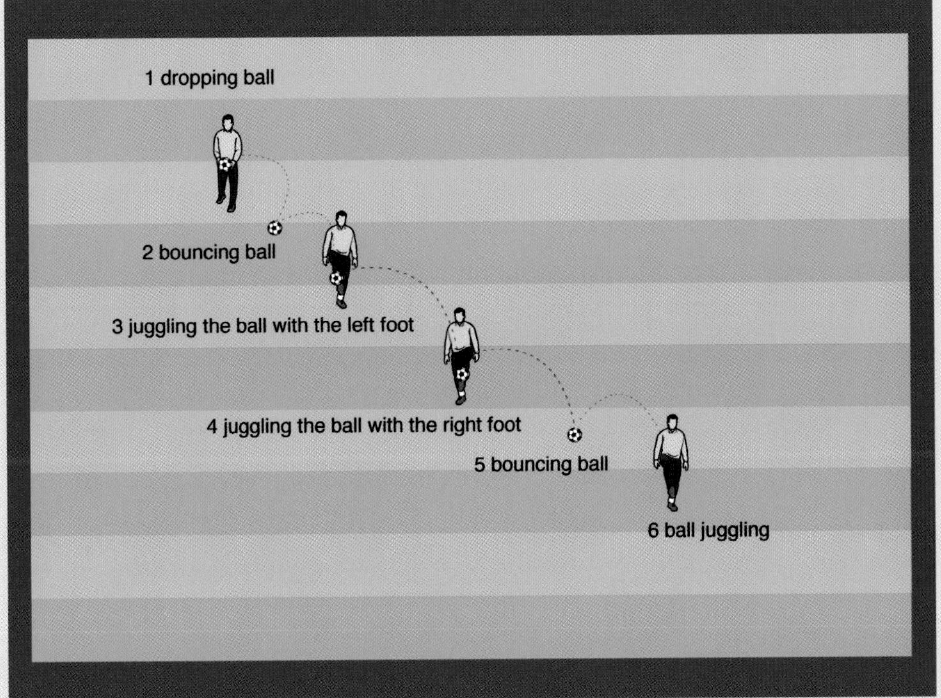

Training Target
- Ball skill (Touch on the ball)

Training Emphasis
- Finesse on the ball
- Lifting the ball
- Juggling techniques
- Coordination

Training Aspects

Skills involved:	Speed of movement with ball, Quick anticipation, Control, Quick decision-making, Quick processing, Combining technical skill with movement, Quickness of reaction Laces, Quick understanding of danger
Age level:	6-8 years, 9-12 years
Level of play:	Beginner
Type of training:	Individual training, Group training
Training structure:	Warm-up, Conclusion, Progression
Purpose:	Improve individual qualities
Total number of players:	2 or more players
Participating players:	Whole team
Training location:	Any
Spatial awareness:	Free space
Duration:	1-10 min

Organization:
One ball per player.

Implementation:
The players take the ball in the hand and throw it in the air. Before the ball touches the ground, the players attempt to keep the ball up with their left and right feet before knocking the ball back into their hands. The players then juggle the ball right/left, etc.

Note:
- The ball should be struck with the laces.
- Both feet should be used one after another.
- The upper body should be held upright, the players should keep their eyes on the ball.
- The standing leg should be slightly bent at the knee.
- The leg playing the ball should also be slightly bent at the knee. The knee should also be raised slightly so that the player's foot is free from the ground.
- The ball should be struck 20-30 cm above the ground.
- The arms remain at the side of the player's body and should be bent at the elbows (similar to the position when carrying buckets of water).
- The ball should not be struck too high into the air.

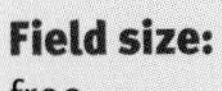

Field size:
free

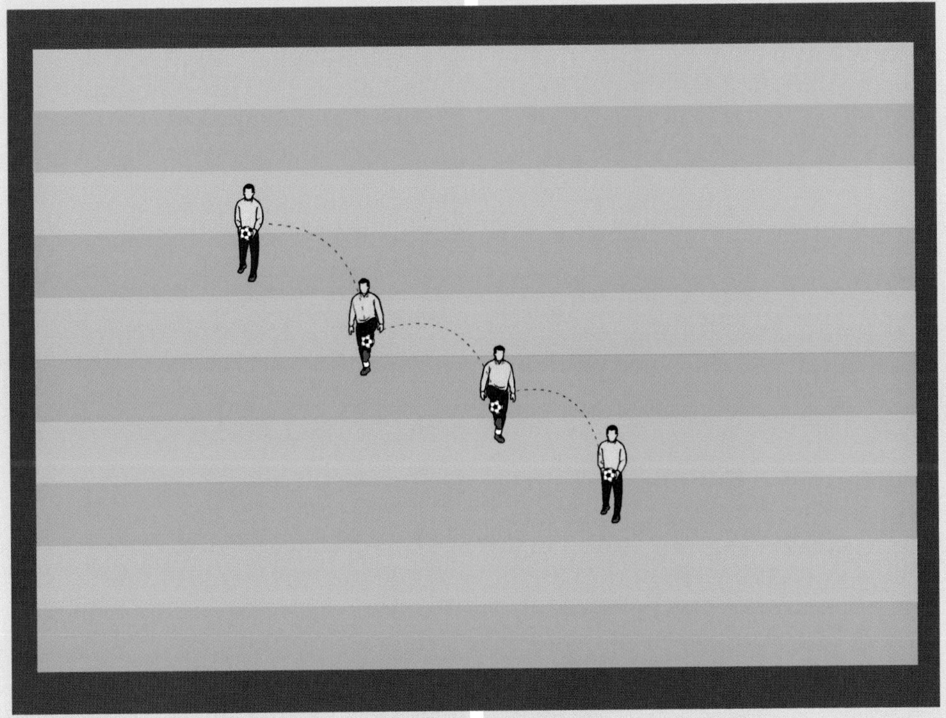

34 Combined Juggling Techniques V

Training Target
- **Ball skill (Touch on the ball)**

Training Emphasis
- **Finesse on the ball**
- **Juggling techniques**
- **Coordination**

Training Aspects

Skills involved:	**Control, Combining technical skill with movement**
Age level:	**6-8 years, 9-12 years**
Level of play:	**Beginner**
Type of training:	**Individual training, Group training**
Training structure:	**Warm-up, Conclusion, Progression**
Purpose:	**Improve individual qualities**
Total number of players:	**2 or more players**
Participating players:	**Whole team**
Training location:	**Any**
Spatial awareness:	**Free space**
Duration:	**1-10 min**

Organization:
One ball per player.

Implementation:
The players take the ball in the hand and drop it onto their thigh and catch the ball again. They alternate this between left and right legs.

Note:
- When the ball strikes the thigh, the leg is bent 90 degrees so that the thigh is flat.
- As the ball strikes the thigh, the player should move his thigh gently upwards to move the ball into the air.
- The standing leg should remain slightly bent.
- The arms remain at the side of the player's body and should be bent at the elbows (similar to the position when carrying buckets of water).
- The player should keep their eyes on the ball.

Field size:
free.

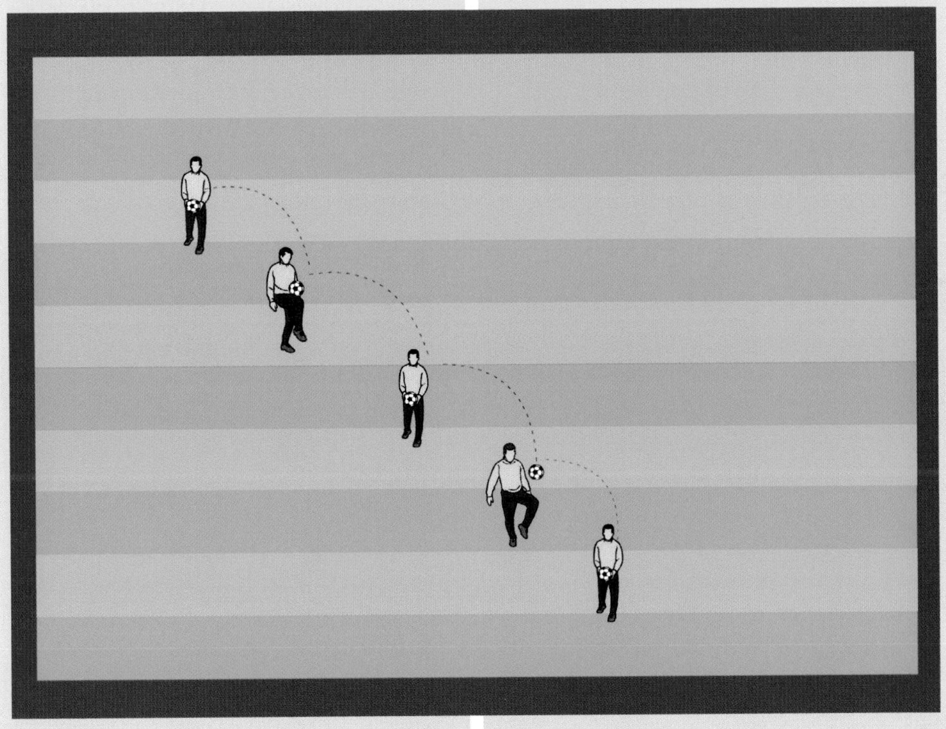

35 Combined Juggling Techniques VI

Training Target
- **Ball skill (Touch on the ball)**

Training Emphasis
- **Finesse on the ball**
- **Juggling techniques**
- **Coordination**

Training Aspects

Skills involved:	Control, Combining technical skill with movement
Age level:	6-8 years, 9-12 years
Level of play:	Beginner
Type of training:	Individual training, Group training
Training structure:	Warm-up, Conclusion, Progression
Purpose:	Improve individual qualities
Total number of players:	2 or more players
Participating players:	Whole team
Training location:	Any
Spatial awareness:	Free space
Duration:	1-10 min

Organization:
One ball per player.

Implementation:
The players take the ball in the hand and drop it onto their thigh alternating between left and right legs. The sequence continues as follows: hand - left thigh - right thigh - hand - right thigh - left thigh - hand, etc.

Note:
- When the ball strikes the thigh, the leg is bent 90 degrees so that the thigh is flat.
- As the ball strikes the thigh, the player should move his thigh gently upwards to move the ball into the air.
- The standing leg should remain slightly bent.
- The arms remain at the side of the player's body and should be bent at the elbows (similar to the position when carrying buckets of water).
- The player should keep their eyes on the ball.

Field size:
free

Training Target
- Ball skill (Touch on the ball)

Training Emphasis
- Finesse on the ball
- Coordination

Training Aspects

Skills involved:	Control, Combining technical skill with movement, Heading from a standstill, Heading while in motion
Age level:	6-8 years, 9-12 years
Level of play:	Beginner
Type of training:	Individual training, Group training
Training structure:	Warm-up, Conclusion, Progression
Purpose:	Improve individual qualities
Total number of players:	2 or more players
Participating players:	Whole team
Training location:	Any
Spatial awareness:	Free space
Duration:	1-10 min

Organization:
One ball per player.

Implementation:
The players throw the ball in the air, head it and then catch the ball. The sequence repeats itself.

Note:
- The players must lean their heads back so that their forehead is level for the ball to strike.
- The ball should be headed with the forehead.
- The players should lean back slightly and keep their eyes on the ball at all times.
- The players' arms should be held slightly away from their body and bent at the elbows (similar to the body position when carrying buckets of water).
- The players closing their eyes shortly before they head the ball is instinctive and completely normal.
- The legs should be slightly bent at the knees. The head is moved upwards towards the ball when the whole body is raised slightly through the knees (similar to the movement in a suspension system). As a result, the ball is headed upwards from the forehead.
- Ensure that the players don't press upwards from their knees too soon, otherwise the ball will be cushioned and cannot be headed upwards. At the same time, if the upwards movement is too hard, then the ball will be headed too high and is then much more difficult to control.

Field size:
free

37 Combined Juggling Techniques VIII

Training Target
- **Ball skill (Touch on the ball)**

Training Emphasis
- **Finesse on the ball**
- **Lifting the ball**
- **Ball control**
- **Juggling techniques**
- **Coordination**

Training Aspects

Skills involved:	Control, Combining technical skill with movement
Age level:	Any age
Level of play:	Recreational
Type of training:	Individual training, Group training
Training structure:	Warm-up, Conclusion, Progression
Purpose:	Training for fun, Improve individual qualities
Total number of players:	2 or more players
Participating players:	Whole team
Training location:	Any
Spatial awareness:	Penalty box
Duration:	5-10 min
Physiology:	Soccer-specific endurance

Organization:
One ball per player.

Implementation:
Free juggling. The players can decide for themselves how they juggle the ball. It is not important whether they allow the ball to touch the ground or not.

Note:
- To introduce a competitive edge, the players can count the number of touches they manage. The player with the most touches is the winner.

Field size:
16-yard box

Training Target
- **Ball skill (Touch on the ball)**

Training Emphasis
- **Juggling techniques**

Training Aspects

Skills involved:	**Control, Combining technical skill with movement, Laces**
Age level:	**Any age**
Level of play:	**Recreational**
Type of training:	**Individual training, Group training**
Training structure:	**Warm-up, Conclusion, Progression**
Purpose:	**Individual training, Improve individual qualities**
Total number of players:	**2 or more players**
Participating players:	**Whole team**
Training location:	**Any**
Spatial awareness:	**Free space**
Duration:	**1-10 min**

Organization:
One ball per player.

Implementation:
The players juggle the ball alternating between the right and the left foot. The ball should be struck with the laces.

Note:
- Most player turn up their toes when hitting the ball. This brings the ball too close to the player's body and brings spin onto the ball. However, this technique is not that hard. That is why we suggest juggling with the laces.
- Juggle with the laces. The player should open their ankles.
- Both feet should be used alternately.
- The upper body should be upright, eyes on the ball.
- The supporting leg should be slightly bent at the knee.
- Non-supporting leg should also be bent at the knee, with the knee slightly raised from the ground so freeing the foot from the ground.
- The ball should be played approx. 20-30 cm from the ground.
- The arms remain at the side of the player's body and should be bent at the elbows (similar to the position when carrying buckets of water).
- The ball shouldn't spin when being juggled (the words on the ball should be visible at all times) => to achieve this it is advisable to stretch out the foot, not to turn the toes up towards the body and to keep the sole of the foot parallel to the floor. Use both feet!

Field size:
free

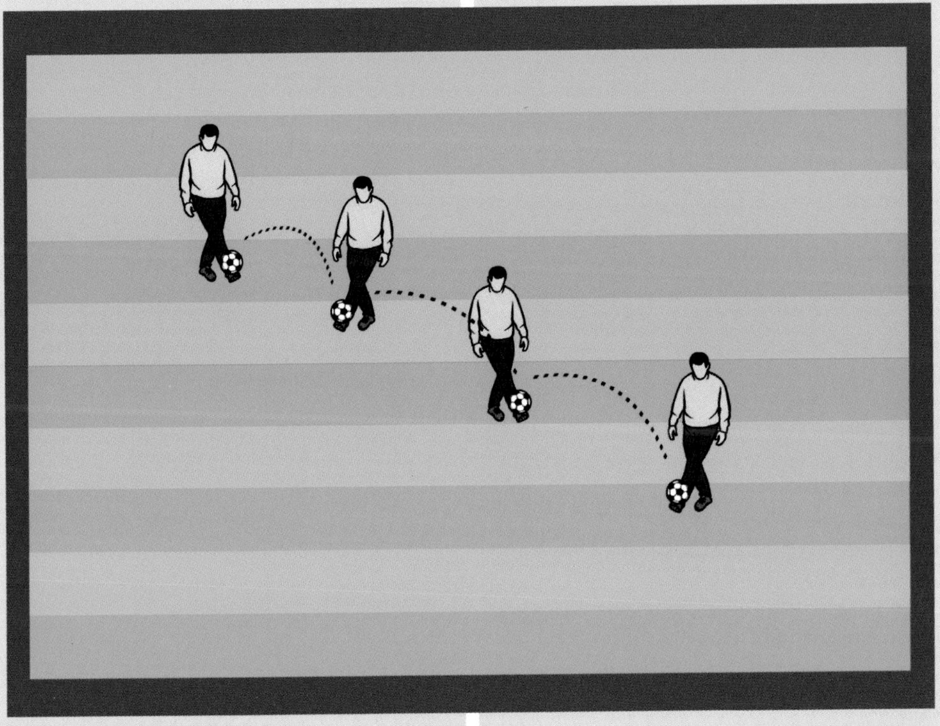

39 Juggling with the Laces - Right/Left

Training Target

- Ball skill (Touch on the ball)

Training Emphasis

- Finesse on the ball
- Lifting the ball
- Juggling techniques
- Coordination

Training Aspects

Skills involved:	Control, Inside of the foot, Combining technical skill with movement, Laces
Age level:	Any age
Level of play:	Recreational
Type of training:	Type of training , Group training
Training structure:	Warm-up, Conclusion, Progression
Purpose:	Improve individual qualities
Total number of players:	2 or more players
Participating players:	Whole team
Training location:	Any
Spatial awareness:	Free space
Duration:	1-10 min

Organization:
One ball per player

Implementation:
The players juggle the ball alternately with the right and the left foot. The ball should be struck using the laces.

Alternative:

- Juggling by trapping the ball between the laces and the ankle (very difficult, requires high skill levels)
- Juggling with toes pointed up (the easiest juggling technique as the ball spins and so is easier to control).

Note:

- Ensure that both feet are used alternately.
- The upper body should be upright with the players' eyes on the ball.
- The standing leg should be slightly bent at the knee.
- The non-supporting leg is also bent at the knee and slightly lifted so that the players' foot is free from the ground.
- The ball should be struck approx. 20-30 cm from the ground.
- The players' ankle should be open, with the toes pointed forwards and the sole of the foot flat.
- Ensure that the ball doesn't hit the toes and that the ball doesn't spin (the words on the ball should be visible at all times).
- The arms remain at the side of the player's body and should be bent at the elbows (similar to the position when carrying buckets of water)
- Juggling the ball with the laces prepares the players for passing, volleying and shooting skills using the laces.

Field size:
free

40 Stage Juggling

Training Target
- Ball skill (Touch on the ball)

Training Emphasis
- Finesse on the ball
- Lifting the ball
- Juggling techniques
- Coordination

Training Aspects

Skills involved:	Control, Combining technical skill with movement, Laces
Age level:	9-12 years, 13- 14 years, 15 years to Adult
Level of play:	Advanced
Type of training:	Individual training
Training structure:	Group training
Purpose:	Improve individual qualities
Total number of players:	2 or more players
Participating players:	Whole team
Training location:	Any
Spatial awareness:	Free space
Duration:	1-10 min
Physiology:	Soccer-specific endurance

Organization:
One ball per player.

Implementation:
The players juggle the ball and steadily increase their number of touches on the ball. The exercise takes the following steps:
1st run-through: juggling, alternating feet
2nd run-through: juggling twice left, twice right
3rd run-through: juggling three times left, three times right
4th run-through: juggling four times left, four times right etc.

Note:
The steps can be followed with all juggling techniques (foot, thigh, head, shoulder, etc.).

Field size:
free

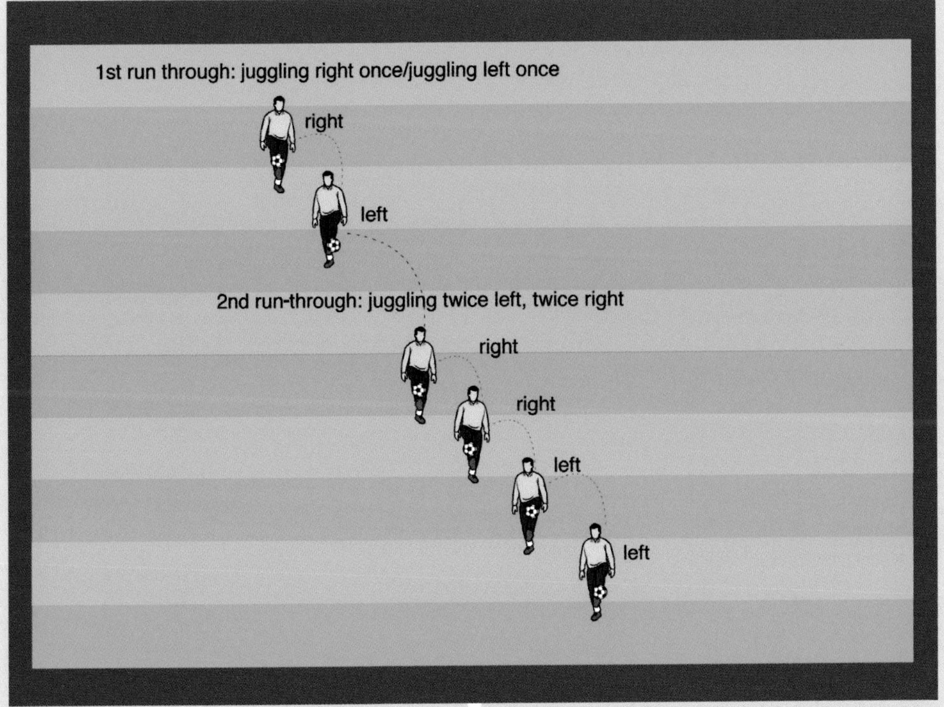

41 Juggling - Knee Left/Right

Training Target
- **Ball skill (Touch on the ball)**

Training Emphasis
- **Finesse on the ball**
- **Lifting the ball**
- **Juggling techniques**

Training Aspects

Skills involved:	**Speed of movement with ball, Control, Combining technical skill with movement**
Age level:	**6-8 years, 9-12 years, 13-14 years, 15-16 years, 15 years to Adult**
Level of play:	**Recreational**
Type of training:	**Individual training, Group training**
Training structure:	**Warm-up, Conclusion, Progression**
Purpose:	**Improve individual qualities**
Total number of players:	**2 or more players**
Participating players:	**Whole team**
Training location:	**Any**
Spatial awareness:	**Free space**
Duration:	**1-10 min**

Organization:
One ball per player.

Implementation:
The players juggle the ball alternately with the left and the right thigh. They are not allowed to touch the ball with any other part of their body.

Alternative:
- Small children should hold the ball in their hands, throw the ball lightly into the air, onto their thigh and then catch it again. Take turns left, right.

Note:
- To introduce a competitive edge, the players can count the number of touches they are able to complete without the ball touching the ground. The player with the most touches wins.
- The thigh must be held flat when the ball touches it (i.e. knee up) so that the ball comes lightly towards the body.
- The player should stand up straight and keep his eye on the ball. The player should be able to lean backwards or forwards to adjust to the flight of the ball.
- The arms remain at the side of the player's body and should be bent at the elbows (similar to the position when carrying buckets of water).

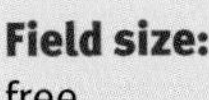

Field size:
free

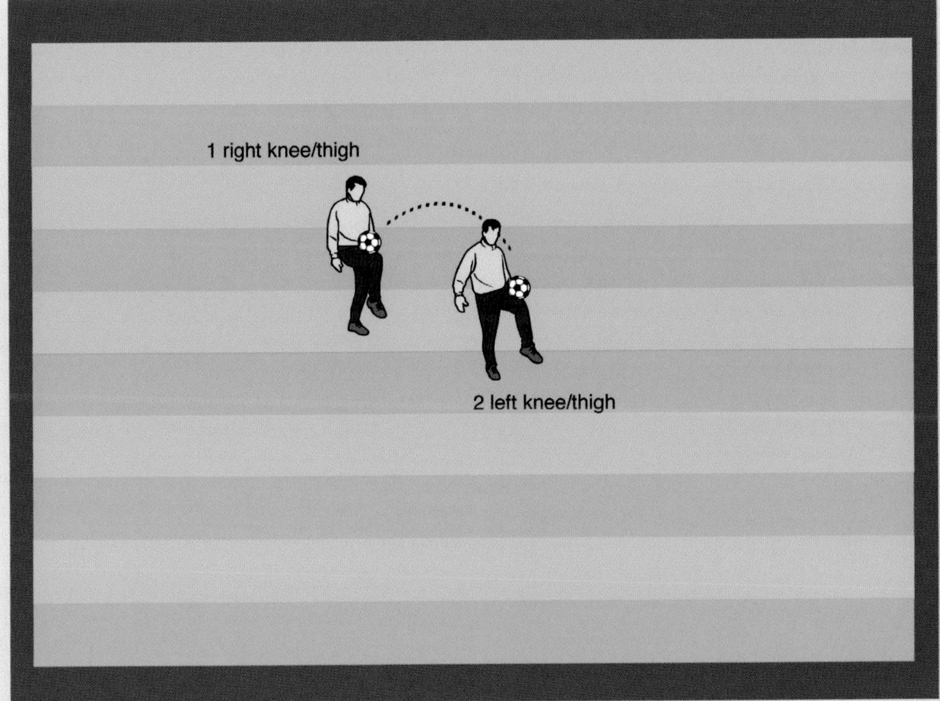

42 Juggling - Head

Training Target
- Ball skill (Touch on the ball)

Training Emphasis
- Finesse on the ball
- Lifting the ball
- Juggling techniques

Training Aspects

Skills involved:	Combining technical skill with movement, Heading from a standstill, Heading while in motion
Age level:	9-12 years, 13-14 years, 15 years to Adult
Level of play:	Recreational
Type of training:	Individual training, Group training
Training structure:	Warm-up, Conclusion, Progression
Purpose:	Improve individual qualities
Total number of players:	2 or more players
Participating players:	Whole team
Training location:	Any
Spatial awareness:	Free space
Duration:	1-10 min

Organization:
One ball per player.

Implementation:
The players juggle the ball on their head, without the ball touching another part of their body.

Note:
- To introduce a competitive edge, the players can count the number of headers they are able to complete without the ball touching the ground. The player with the most headers wins.
- The player has to lean his head back so that his forehead is flat, so that the ball can bounce straight up.
- The ball should be headed with the forehead.
- The player should lean back slightly and keep his eye on the ball.
- The arms remain at the side of the player's body and should be bent at the elbows (similar to the position when carrying buckets of water)
- That the players close their eyes shortly before they head the ball is instinctive and completely normal.
- The legs should be slightly bent at the knees. The head is moved upwards towards the ball when the whole body is raised slightly through the knees (similar to the movement in a suspension system). As a result, the ball is headed upwards from the forehead.
- Ensure that the players don't press upwards from their knees too soon, otherwise the ball will be cushioned and cannot be headed upwards. At the same time, if the upwards movement is too hard then the ball will be headed too high and is then much more difficult to control.

Field size:
free

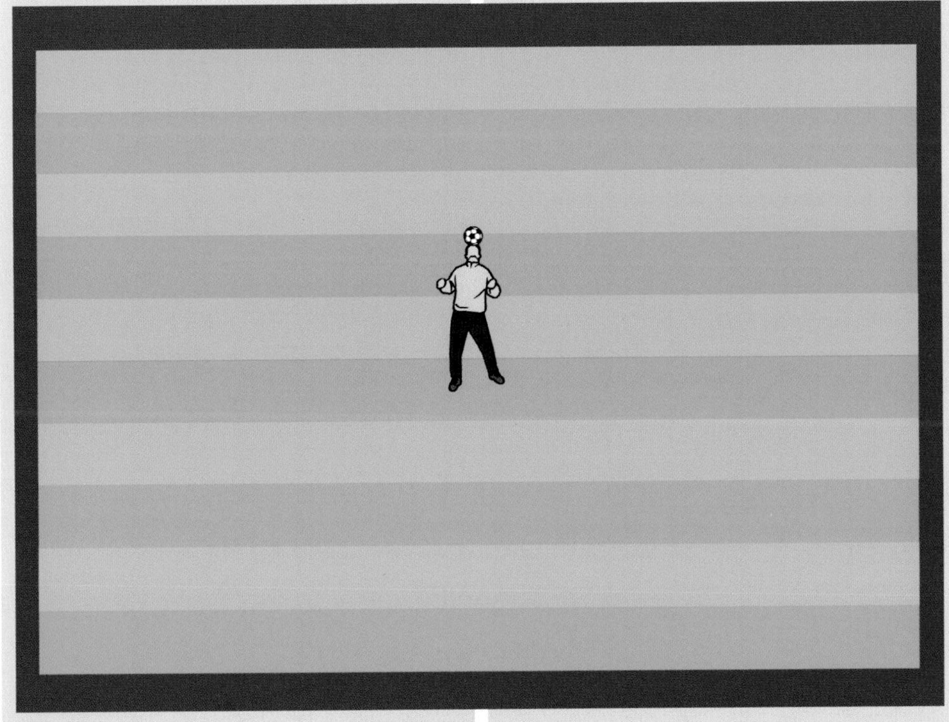

43 Juggling - Foot Left/Knee Left, Foot Right/Knee Right

Training Target
- **Ball skill (Touch on the ball)**

Training Emphasis
- **Finesse on the ball**
- **Lifting the ball**
- **Juggling techniques**
- **Coordination**

Training Aspects

Skills involved:	Control, Inside of the foot, Combining technical skill with movement, Quickness of reaction, Laces
Age level:	9-12 years, 13-14 years, 15 years to Adult
Level of play:	Advanced
Type of training:	Individual training, Group training
Training structure:	Warm-up, Conclusion, Progression
Purpose:	Improve individual qualities
Total number of players:	2 or more players, Single Player
Participating players:	Whole team
Training location:	Any
Spatial awareness:	Free space
Duration:	1-10 min

Organization:
One ball per player.

Process:
The players juggle the ball in the following order: left foot, left knee/thigh, right foot, and right knee/thigh. After touching the right knee/thigh, the ball moves on to the left foot and the run-through starts all over again.

Tip:
- The players should only touch the ball once with each part of their body.
- To introduce a competitive edge, the players can count the number of touches they are able to complete without the ball touching the ground. The player with the most touches wins.

Field size:
free

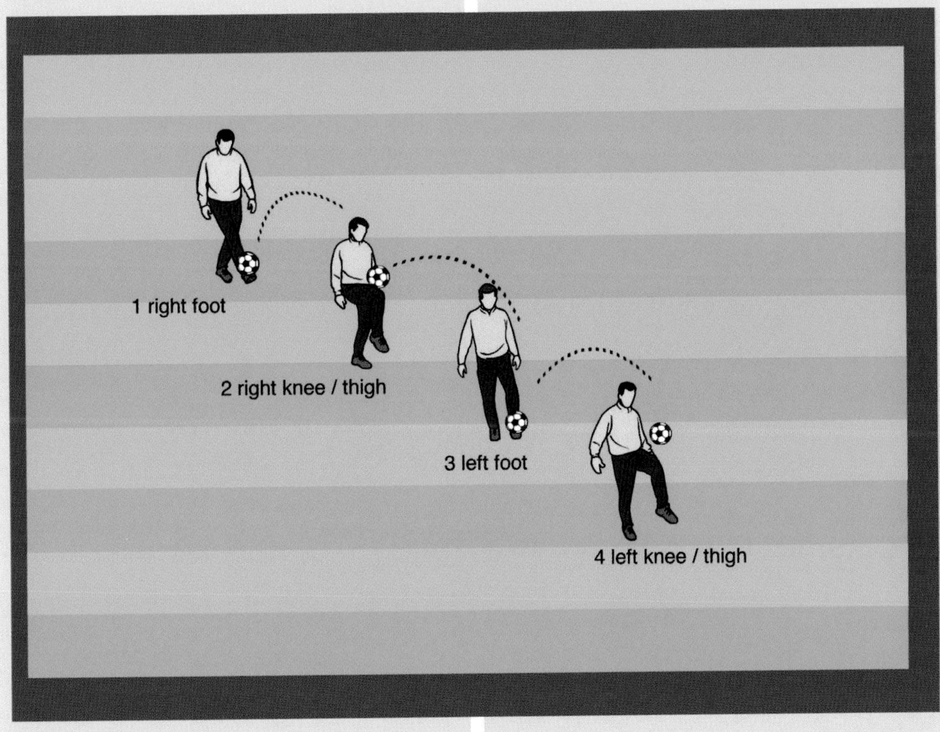

44 Juggling - Foot, Head, Knee

Training Target
- **Ball skill (Touch on the ball)**

Training Emphasis
- **Finesse on the ball**
- **Lifting the ball**
- **Juggling techniques**

Training Aspects

Skills involved:	**Quick anticipation, Control, Quick decision-making, Combining technical skill with movement, Heading from a standstill, Laces**
Age level:	**9- 12 years, 13- 14 years, 15 years to Adult**
Level of play:	**Advanced**
Type of training:	**Individual training, Group training**
Training structure:	**Warm-up, Conclusion, Progression**
Purpose:	**Improve individual qualities**
Total number of players:	**2 or more players**
Participating players:	**Whole team**
Training location:	**Any**
Spatial awareness:	**Free space**
Duration:	**1-10 min**

Organization:
One ball per player.

Implementation:
The players juggle the ball in the following order: foot, head, knee. After each run-through the players change legs (right foot, head, right knee, left foot, head, left knee, etc.).

Note:
- The players should only touch the ball once with each part of their body.
- To introduce a competitive edge, the players can count the number of touches they are able to complete without the ball touching the ground. The player with the most touches wins.
- This exercise requires close skill levels and high levels of coordination.

Field size:
free

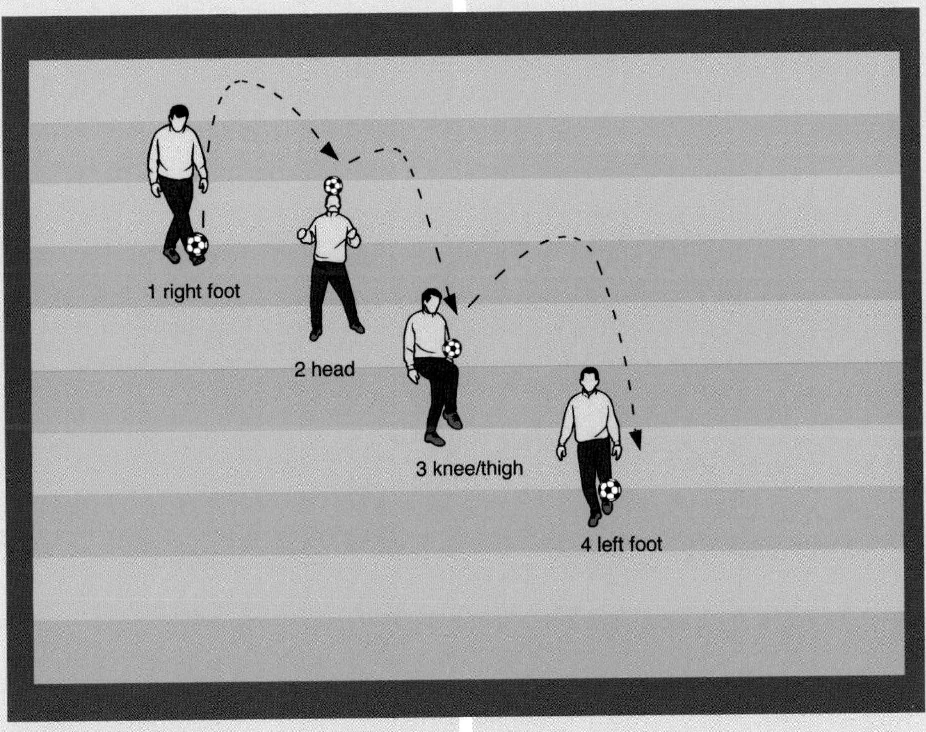

45 Juggling - Foot/Knee/Shoulder/Head/Shoulder/Knee/Foot

Training Target
- Ball skill (Touch on the ball)

Training Emphasis
- Finesse on the ball
- Lifting the ball
- Juggling techniques

Training Aspects

Skills involved:	Speed of movement with ball, Quick anticipation, Control, Trapping into space, Quick decision-making, Inside of the foot, Combining technical skill with movement, Heading from a standstill, Quickness of reaction, Laces
Age level:	13-14 years, 15 years to Adult
Level of play:	Professional
Type of training:	Individual training, Group training
Training structure:	Warm-up, Conclusion, Progression
Purpose:	Improve individual qualities
Total number of players:	2 or more players
Participating players:	Whole team
Training location:	Any
Spatial awareness:	Free space
Duration:	1-10 min

Organization:
One ball per player.

Implementation:
The players juggle the ball in the following order: right foot, right knee, right shoulder, head, left shoulder, left knee and left foot. Then left foot, left knee, left shoulder, head, right shoulder, right knee, right foot. The sequence then starts again.

Note:
- The players should only touch the ball once with each part of their body.
- To introduce a competitive edge, the players can count the number of touches they are able to complete without the ball touching the ground. The player with the most touches wins.
- This exercise requires high skill levels and high levels of coordination.

Field size:
free

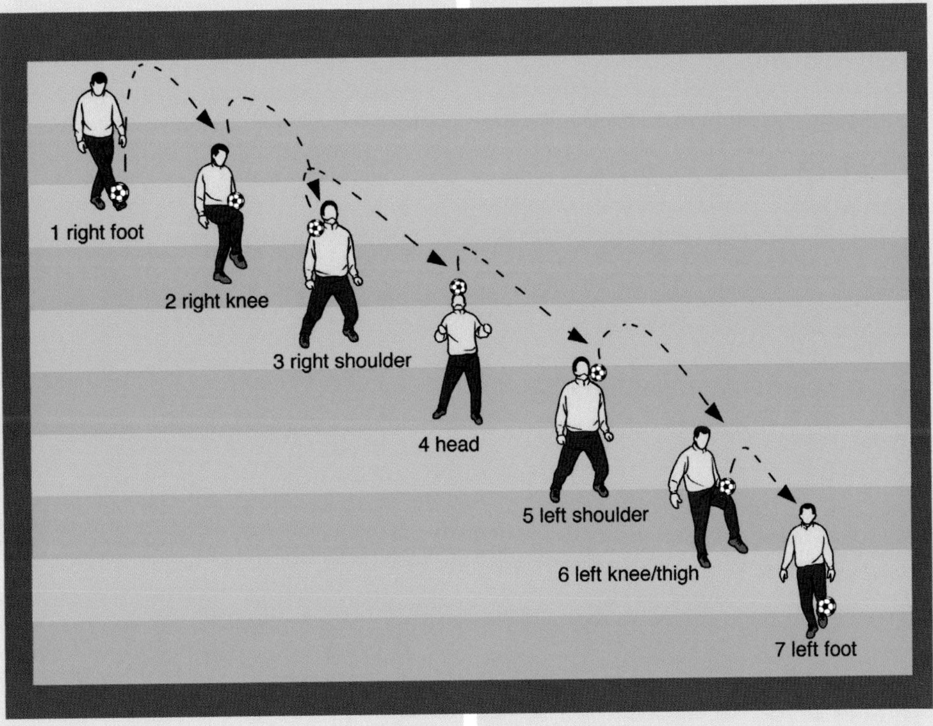

46 Juggling - Left Foot Over the Head, Right Foot Over the Head

Training Target

- Ball skill (Touch on the ball)

Training Emphasis

- Finesse on the ball
- Lifting the ball
- Juggling techniques
- Coordination

Training Aspects

Skills involved:	Quick anticipation, Control, Inside of the foot, Combining technical skill with movement, Quickness of reaction, Volley, Laces
Age level:	13-14 years, 15 years to Adult
Level of play:	Age level
Type of training:	Advanced
Training structure:	Warm-up, Conclusion, Progression
Purpose:	Improve individual qualities
Total number of players:	2 or more players
Participating players:	Whole team
Training location:	Any
Spatial awareness:	Free space
Duration:	1-10 min
Physiology:	Soccer-specific endurance

Organization:
One ball per player.

Implementation:
The players juggle the ball then hit the ball over their head with their left foot, spin 180 degrees, hit the ball back over their head with their right foot. The players then repeat this sequence.

Note:

- The players lift the ball over their head with their laces. The players' ankles should be open, with the toes pointed forwards and the sole of the foot flat. The players' leg should be bent at the knee.
- The players should turn 180 degrees immediately after hitting the ball over their heads. To do this, they should place their foot which just struck the ball firmly on the ground and spin quickly on that foot, turning their whole upper body.

Field size:
free

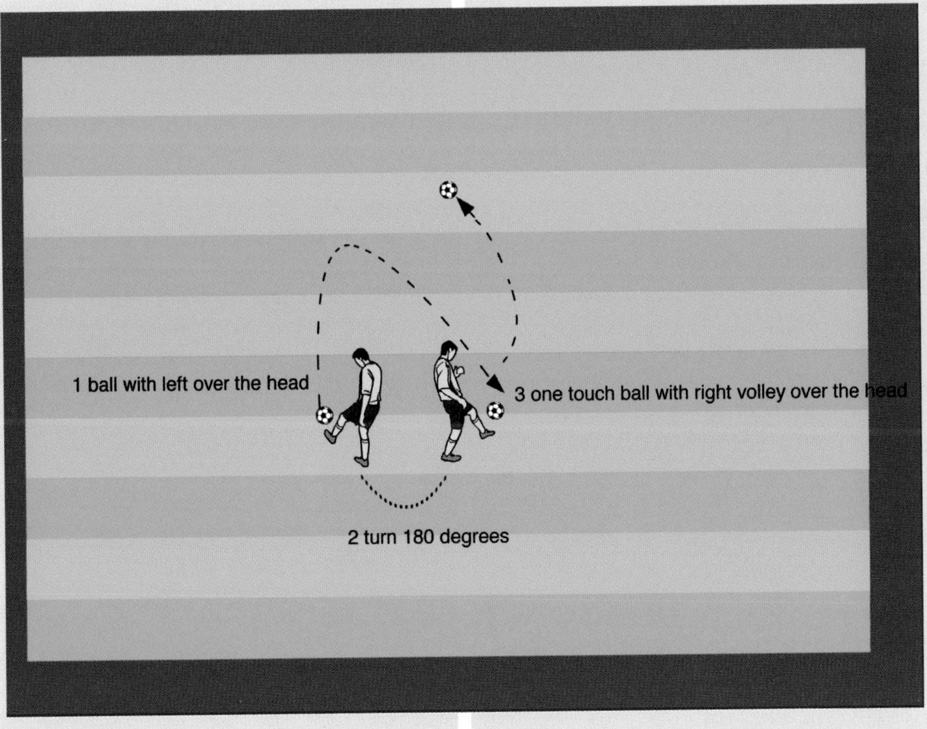

47 Juggling - Left Foot Right Heel, Right Foot Left Heel

Training Target
- **Ball skill (Touch on the ball)**

Training Emphasis
- **Finesse on the ball**
- **Lifting the ball**
- **Juggling techniques**

Training Aspects

Skills involved:	**Speed of movement with ball, Control, Inside of the foot, Combining technical skill with movement, Laces**
Age level:	**13-14 years, 15-16 years, 17 years to Adult**
Level of play:	**Advanced, Professional**
Type of training:	**Individual training, Group training**
Training structure:	**Warm-up, Conclusion, Progression**
Purpose:	**Improve individual qualities**
Total number of players:	**2 or more players**
Participating players:	**Whole team**
Training location:	**Any**
Spatial awareness:	**Free space**
Duration:	**1-10 min**

Organization:
One ball per player.

Implementation:
The players juggle the ball alternately with their left foot, right heel to their right foot and then onto their left heel. The sequence then begins from the start again.

Alternative: The ball can also be juggled using the outstep instead of the heel.

Note:
- In order to strike the ball with the heel, the players have to take a short step forwards after knocking the ball in the air in order to put themselves in front of the ball. As a result, the players free up their other leg (in this case their right) to back heel the ball in the air. The players must duck on one leg slightly and turn their upper body towards the ball to successfully strike the ball with the heel. The players then find themselves in their original positions.
- The players should keep their eyes on the ball at all times.
- The ball must strike the ankle on the Achilles because the heel has a very small surface area.
- To juggle the ball with the outstep, the player will have to turn their lower leg outwards at the knee. The upper body should alternate between leaning to the opposite side to balance the player and standing up straight. The players' ankles should be open.
- This skill is challenging and should only be attempted with advanced players.

Field size:
free

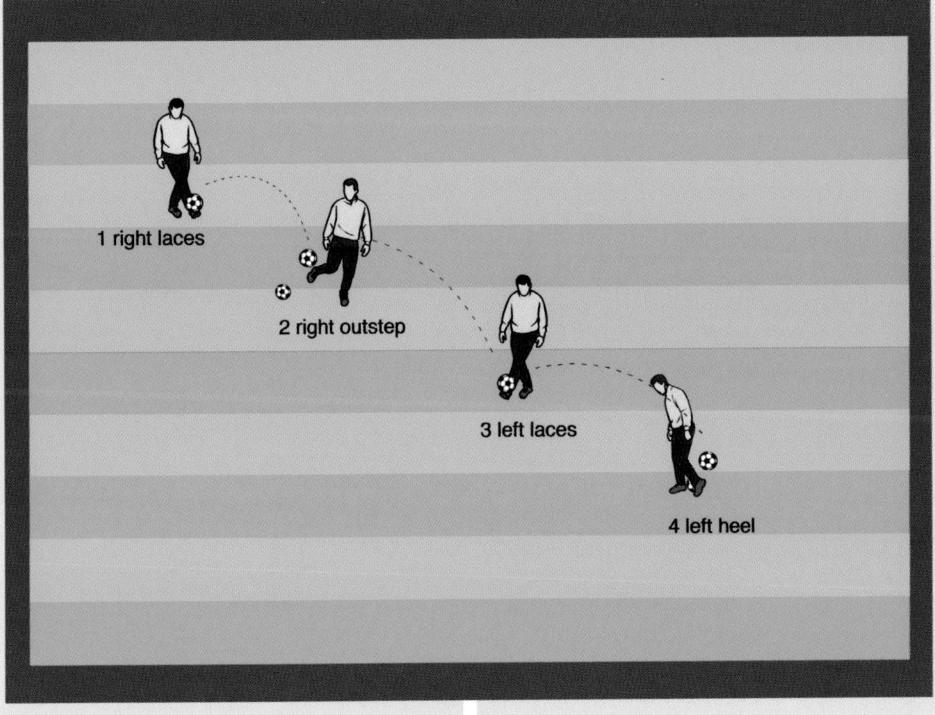

48 Juggling - Foot, Head, Chest, Knee

Training Target

- **Ball skill (Touch on the ball)**

Training Emphasis

- **Finesse on the ball**
- **Lifting the ball**
- **Juggling techniques**

Training Aspects

Skills involved:	**Quick anticipation, Control, Quick decision-making, Combining technical skill with movement, Heading from a standstill, Laces**
Age level:	**9-12 years, 13- 14 years, 15 years to Adult**
Level of play:	**Advanced**
Type of training:	**Individual training, Group training**
Training structure:	**Warm-up, Conclusion, Progression**
Purpose:	**Improve individual qualities**
Total number of players:	**2 or more players**
Participating players:	**Whole team**
Training location:	**Any**
Spatial awareness:	**Free space**
Duration:	**1-10 min**

Organization:
One ball per player.

Implementation:
The players juggle the ball in the following order: foot, head, chest and knee. The player juggles the ball from their foot up onto their head, lets it drop onto their chest and then onto their thigh. From here the player lets the ball drop down to his feet (the other foot) and the sequence begins again (using the other side of his body). After each run-through the player should change feet/knees (right, left, right, left, etc.).

Note:
- The players should only touch the ball once with each part of their body.
- To introduce a competitive edge, the players can count the number of touches they are able to complete without the ball touching the ground. The player with the most touches wins.
- This exercise requires extremely high skill levels and high levels of coordination.

Field size:
free

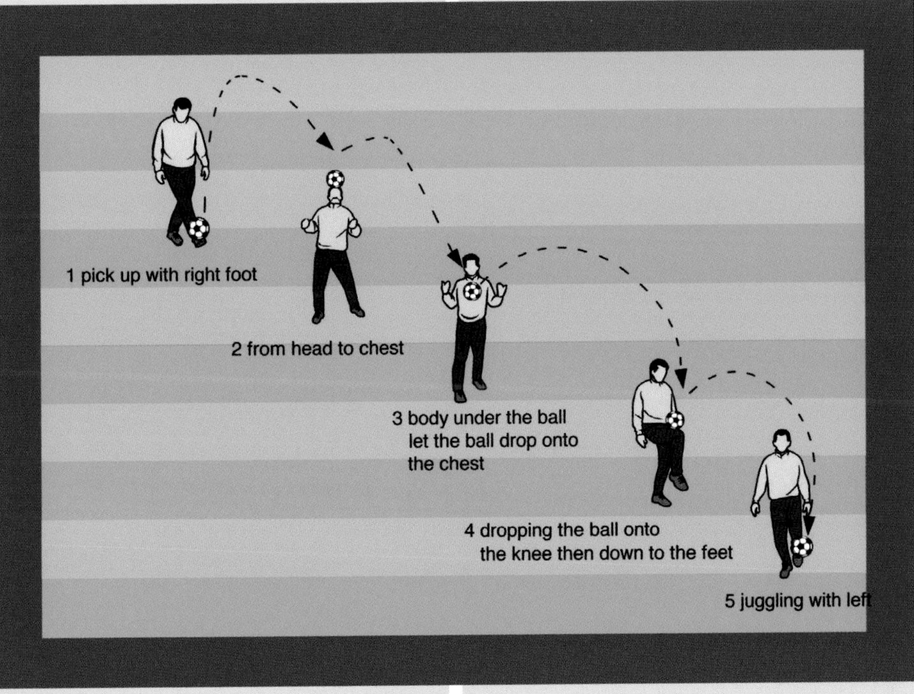

49 Juggling - Foot, Knee, Head, Neck, Heel, Chest

Training Target
- **Ball skill (Touch on the ball)**

Training Emphasis
- **Juggling techniques**

Training Aspects

Skills involved:	Quick anticipation, Control, Quick processing, Combining technical skill with movement, Heading from a standstill, Laces
Age level:	13-14 years, 15 years to Adult
Level of play:	Professional
Type of training:	Individual training, Group training
Training structure:	Warm-up, Conclusion, Progression
Purpose:	Improve individual qualities
Total number of players:	2 or more players
Participating players:	Whole team
Training location:	Any
Spatial awareness:	Free space
Duration:	1-10 min

Organization:
One ball per player.

Implementation:
The players juggle the ball in the following order: foot, knee, head, neck, heel and chest. The player then lets the ball drop from his chest onto his foot and the sequence starts again. After each run-through the player should change feet (right, left, right, left, etc.).

Note:
- This juggling sequence is very difficult and so only suitable for players/teams with advanced skills.
- This exercise requires extremely high skill levels and high levels of coordination.

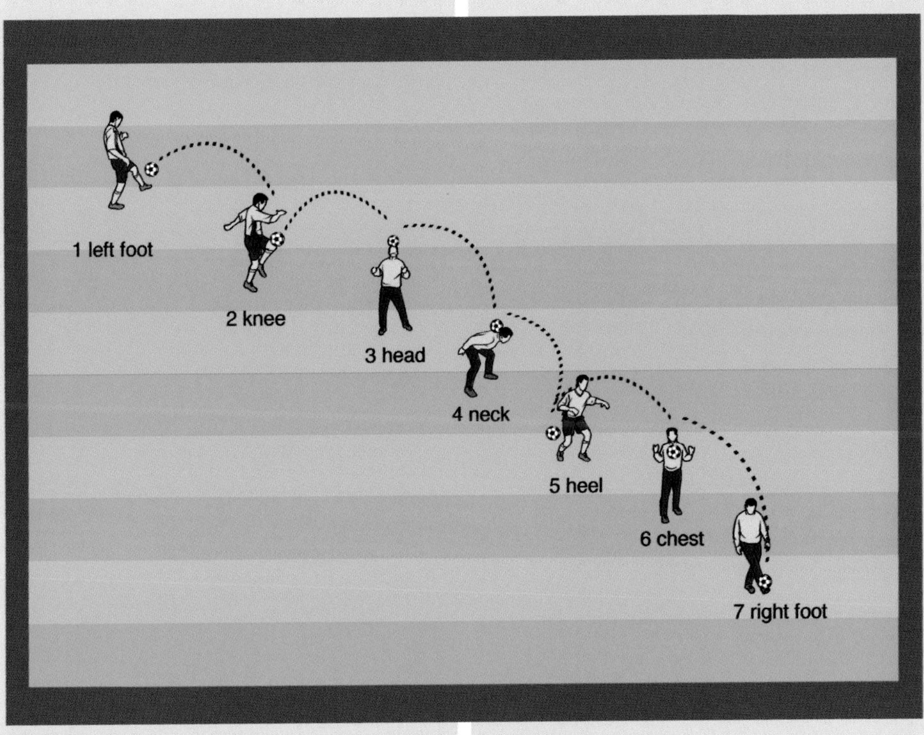
1 left foot
2 knee
3 head
4 neck
5 heel
6 chest
7 right foot

50 Ball Juggling in Threes

Training Target
- **Ball skill (Touch on the ball)**

Training Emphasis
- **Finesse on the ball**
- **Lifting the ball**
- **Juggling techniques**

Training Aspects	
Skills involved:	Trapping, Control, Flexibility, One touch passes, Quick decision-making, Inside of the foot, Combining technical skill with movement, Passing over multiple stations
Age level:	13-14 years, 15-16 years, 15 years to Adult
Level of play:	Advanced, Professional
Type of training:	Group training
Training structure:	Warm-up, Progression
Purpose:	Improve individual qualities
Total number of players:	3 players
Participating players:	Whole team
Training location:	Any
Spatial awareness:	Limited playing field
Duration:	10-15 min
Physiology:	Soccer-specific endurance

Organization:
2 cones laid out opposite to one another. 3 players. One ball.

Implementation:
Three players keep the ball in the air and pass to one another.

Alternative:
- The player with the ball calls out the number of touches the next player can take as the ball leaves his foot (1, 2, 2 or 3).
- Juggling in threes. Restrict to: foot only, head only, knee only.
- The player remains in the middle and turns to lay the ball off to the next player.
- Follow the pass. Players permanently change their positions.

Note:
- Open the foot when passing with the laces.
- If possible pull the toes up to put spin on the ball which makes it easy to juggle. As a result, the fine skills are coached less.
- Communication.
- Instep, outstep and laces, knee, head, chest, shoulders can also be used.
- Don't pass too hard.

Field size:
5 x 10 m.

Distance between the cones:
10 m

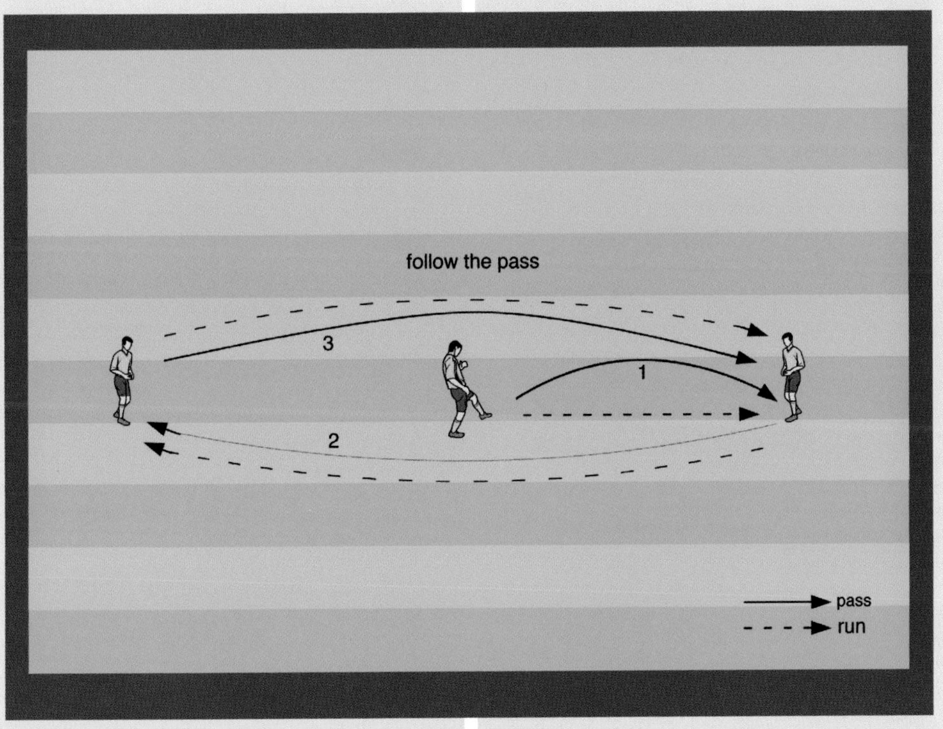

51 Juggling Variations

Training Target

- **Ball skill (Touch on the ball)**

Training Emphasis

- **Finesse on the ball**
- **Lifting the ball**
- **Juggling techniques**
- **Coordination**

Training Aspects

Skills involved:	Control, Combining technical skill with movement
Age level:	13-14 years
Level of play:	Advanced, Professional
Type of training:	Group training
Training structure:	Warm-up, Progression
Purpose:	Improve individual qualities
Total number of players:	6 or more players
Participating players:	Whole team
Training location:	any
Spatial awareness:	Penalty box
Duration:	10-20 min
Physiology:	Soccer-specific endurance

Organization:
All players should have a ball in the 18-yard box.

Implementation:
The players spread out in the 18-yard box and move the ball using the different juggling techniques called out from the coach. The following juggling techniques are available: Left right alternating- Foot left/right, knee left/right- Foot/head/knee alternating left/right- Head- Knee left/right- Foot/knee/shoulder/head/shoulder/knee/foot- Left foot over the head, right foot over the head- Left foot right heel, right foot left heel- Laces right/left- Foot, head, chest, knee- Foot, knee, head, neck, heel, chest.

Note:

- The players should regularly raise their heads to avoid colliding with the other players.
- Requires a high level of concentration.
- The players shouldn't strike the ball too hard.
- Players should adjust their body to compensate for the differing flight of the ball.
- The players' toes should not be pointed upwards.
- The players should not lean back too much.

Competition: Who can keep the ball up the longest?

- These juggling techniques are intended for a group of players of advanced level.

Field size:
18-yard box

52 Juggling in a Box

Training Target
- Ball skill (Touch on the ball)

Training Emphasis
- Finesse on the ball
- Lifting the ball
- Juggling techniques
- Coordination

Training Aspects

Skills involved:	Control, Combining technical skill with movement
Age level:	Any age
Level of play:	Recreational
Type of training:	Group training
Training structure:	Warm-up, Conclusion, Progression
Purpose:	Improve individual qualities
Total number of players:	2 or more players
Participating players:	Whole team
Training location:	Any
Spatial awareness:	Limited playing field
Duration:	5-15 min
Physiology:	Soccer-specific endurance

Organization:
Each player starts in his own box with a ball.

Implementation:
The players juggle in their box. They can either choose which juggling technique they use or can follow the skills called out by the coach.

Note:
- Ensure that both feet are used alternately.
- The upper body should be upright with the players' eyes on the ball.
- The standing leg should be slightly bent at the knee.
- The non-supporting leg is also bent at the knee and slightly lifted so that the players' foot is free from the ground.
- The arms remain at the side of the player's body and should be bent at the elbows (similar to the position when carrying buckets of water).
- The ball should not be struck too high into the air (max. head height).

Field size:
Variable, e.g. 5 x 5 m

Distance between the cones:
Variable, e.g. 5 meters wide; 5 m long.

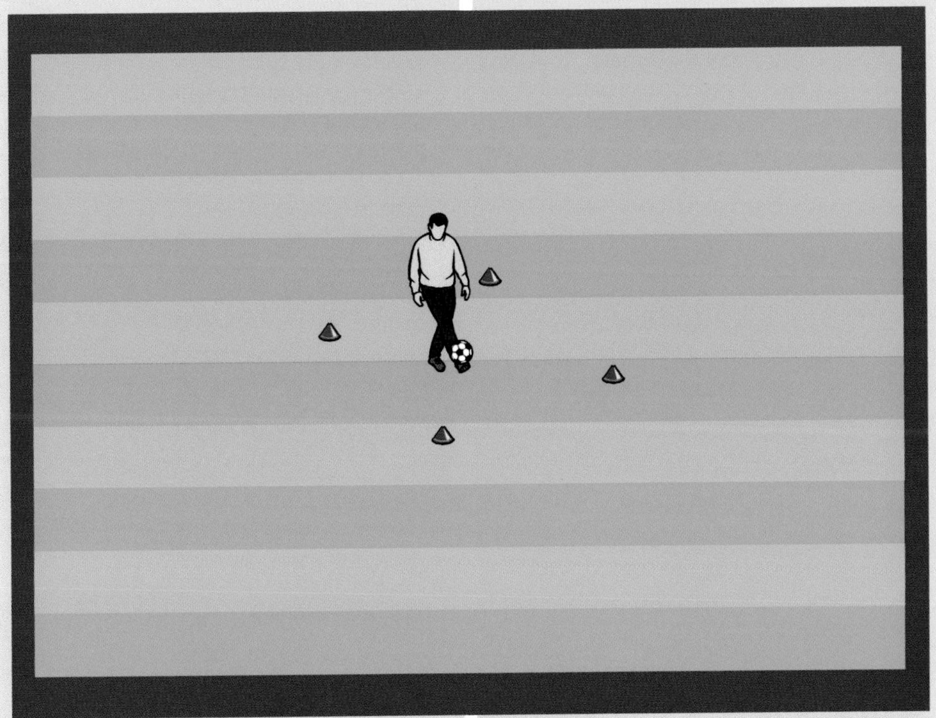

53 Juggling in a Box + Volley-Shot at Goal

Training Target
- Ball skill (Touch on the ball)
- Goalkeepers

Training Emphasis
- Finesse on the ball
- Lifting the ball
- Explosiveness
- Juggling techniques
- Coordination
- Shooting

Training Aspects

Skills involved:	Control, Quick decision-making, Combining technical skill with movement, Volley, Laces
Age level:	9-12 years, 13-14 years, 15 years to Adult
Level of play:	Advanced
Type of training:	Individual training, Group training
Training structure:	Progression, Main point/Emphasis
Purpose:	Improve individual qualities
Total number of players:	2 or more players
Participating players:	Whole team
Training location:	Any
Spatial awareness:	Limited playing field
Duration:	10-20 min
Goalkeeping:	1-3 goalies

Organization:
Set up one or more boxes with a goal 15-20 meters from each box. One ball per player.

Implementation:
One player juggles in each box. The remaining players spread themselves out over the other boxes and wait for their go. After a given number of touches, or after the call from the coach, the players volley the ball from their box into the goal and leave the box to collect their ball. The next player enters the box and starts the same sequence again.

Note:
- Various juggling/combinations can be used (e.g. juggling only with the laces; alternating foot/knee; step juggling (1 x right, 1 x left, 2 x right, 2 x left etc.).
- To ensure that the drill runs fluidly, it is advisable to setup several boxes, depending upon the size of the group.
- The exercise can also be set up in the form of a competition - every player has to count how many goals he scores. The coach can also implement the rule that a player is not allowed to take a shot if his ball falls to the ground. The players should complete a set number of drills.
- The players' upper body should be slightly bent forwards when volleying the ball which should be struck at a low point (not too high). Only in this way can the players control correctly and put the right weight on the ball.

Field size:
Box ca. 5 x 5 m + goal 15-20 m away.

Distance between the cones:
5 m wide, 5 m long.

54 Juggling, Volleyed Pass + Shot at Goal I

Training Target
- **Ball skill (Touch on the ball)**

Training Emphasis
- **Lifting the ball**
- **Juggling techniques**
- **Coordination**
- **Shooting**

Training Aspects

Skills involved:	Speed of movement with ball, Quick anticipation, Wall passes, Quick decision-making, Quick processing, Inside of the laces passing, Combining technical skill with movement, Quickness of reaction, Volley
Age level:	13-14 years, 15 years to Adult
Level of play:	Advanced, Professional
Type of training:	Group training
Training structure:	Main point/Emphasis
Purpose:	Attack behavior, Improve individual qualities
Total number of players:	4 or more players
Participating players:	Whole team
Training location:	Any
Spatial awareness:	Limited playing field
Duration:	10-20 min
Physiology:	Soccer-specific endurance
Goalkeeping:	1 goalie

Organization:
Set up a goal and a start cone and a layoff cone for the players. One ball per player. Goalkeepers in goal.

Implementation:
The players juggle, on the move, 2-4 times and then pass to the red player. The red player hits the ball first time sideways or to the back and side. The blue player must finish, with a volley the first time.

Note:
- Concentration is required with this technically demanding skill.
- The ball should not be struck too high.
- The timing of the pass and high precision in the pass are required.

Field size:
20 x 20 m

Distance between the cones:
10 m

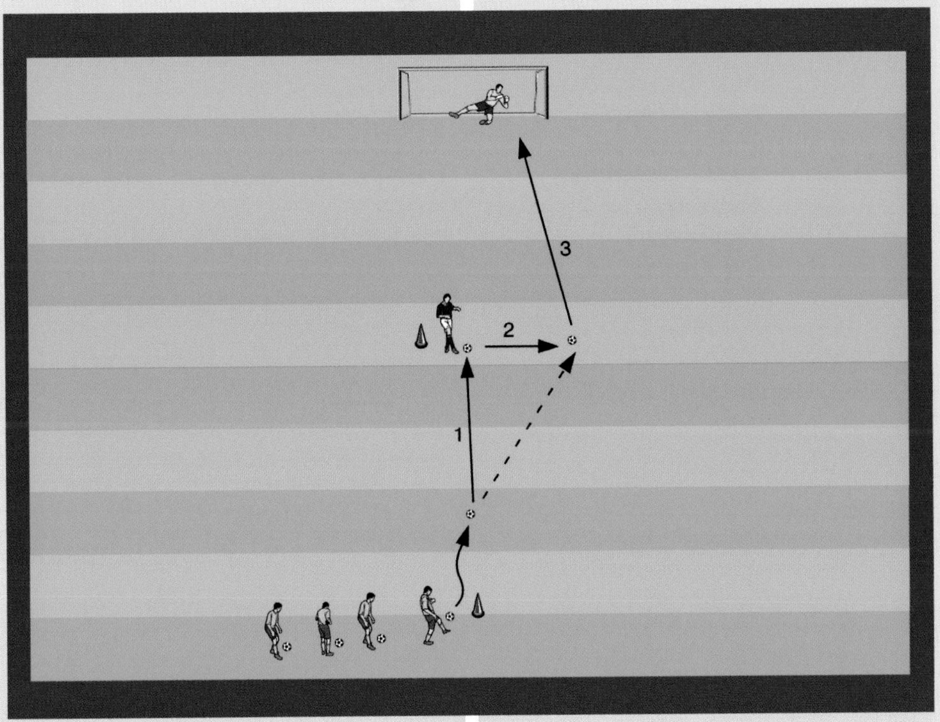

55 Juggling, Volleyed Pass + Shot at Goal II

Training Target
- Ball skill (Touch on the ball)

Training Emphasis
- Finesse on the ball
- Fun games
- Quick transitioning (defense to offense) (Countering)
- Quick transitioning (offense to defense) (Getting back)

Training Aspects

Skills involved:	Speed of movement with ball, Control, Speed of movement off the ball, Quick decision-making, Quick processing, Inside of the foot passing, Inside of the laces passing, Combining technical skill with movement, Counter-attacks, Header challenges, Heading from a jump, Short passing, Long passing, Passing over multiple stations, Quickness of reaction, Direct play to the forwards, Opening the field from the goalie, Volley, Laces, Quick understanding of danger
Age level:	17 years to Adult
Level of play:	Professional
Type of training:	Team training
Training structure:	Warm-up, Progression, Main point/Emphasis
Purpose:	Training for fun, Cooperation within the team, Improve individual qualities
Total number of players:	12 players, 13 or more players
Participating players:	Whole team
Training location:	Indoor, Asphalt, Turf field, Grass field
Spatial awareness:	Limited playing field, Double penalty box
Duration:	15-20 min
Physiology:	Soccer-specific endurance
Goalkeeping:	2 goalies

Organization:
Set up a playing area with two goals. Several balls in one goal. The coach selects two teams of 6-9 players.

Implementation:
Two teams, both with goalkeepers. The ball can only be controlled in the air. If the ball touches the ground, the opposing team gains possession. The team without the ball is allowed to attack the team in possession and attempt to regain possession. Only the goalkeeper is allowed to touch the ball with his hands. If the ball touches the ground, the nearest player can volley pass the ball from his hands from that position. The player in possession is allowed as many touches as he likes. Only goals scored directly (with the players' first touch/volley) count.

Alternative:
- Only 1, 2 or 3 touch(es) allowed.
- The ball can be caught, but can only be passed as a volley.

Note:

- The game often flows better when the goalkeeper makes a long, up field clearance.
- When possible, the players should play one touch.
- The teams should be set out according to their positions (to avoid all the players gathering forward or at the back).
- This is a game for highly skilled players/teams.

Field size:

30 x 20 m

Distance between the cones:

Length: 15 m each (3 cones) Width: 20 m

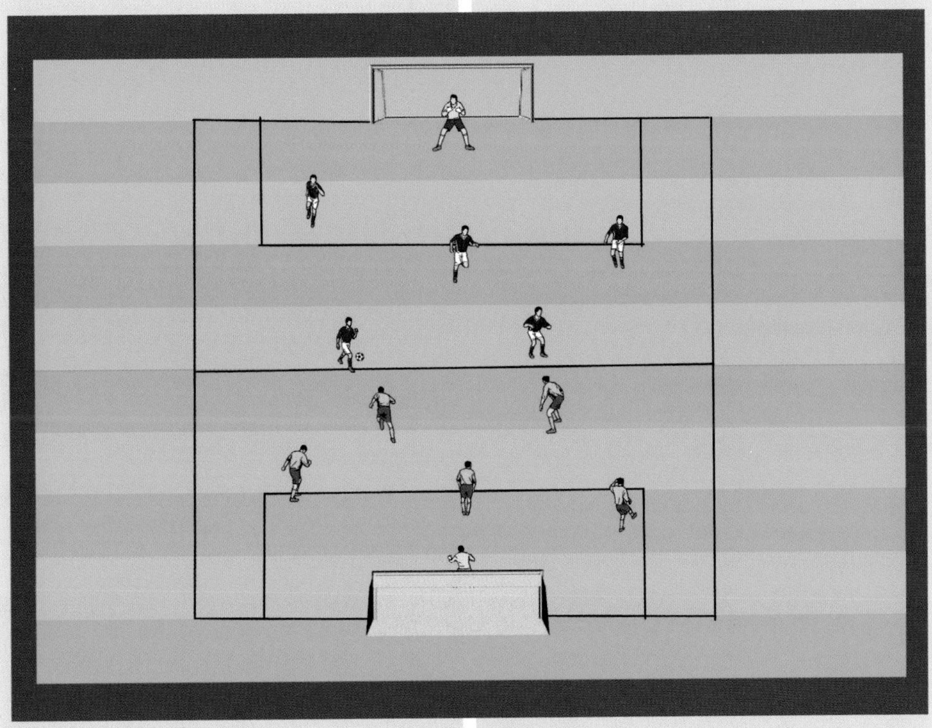

Training Target
- Ball skill (Touch on the ball)

Training Emphasis
- Dribbling control
- Finesse on the ball
- Feinting/trick dribbling
- Fitness program

Training Aspects

Skills involved:	Speed of movement with ball, Quick anticipation, Dribbling, Quick decisioning, Quick processing, Bodyfake, Combining technical skill with movement, Quickness of reaction, Quick understanding of danger
Age level:	6-8 years, 9-12 years, 13-14 years, 15 years to Adult
Level of play:	Advanced
Type of training:	Group training, Team training
Training structure:	Warm-up, Progression
Purpose:	Improve individual qualities
Total number of players:	6 or more players
Participating players:	Whole team
Training location:	Any
Spatial awareness:	Penalty box
Duration:	10-30 min
Physiology:	Soccer-specific endurance, Training of elementary endurance II, Strength, Speed endurance, Power & Speed

Organization:
Each player has a ball in the 18-yard box.

Implementation:
The players assemble in the 18-yard box and start dribbling with the ball and following the coach's commands.
This could include the following skills:
- dummy-flick with the instep/outstep
- step over (standing, on the move, with an opponent)
- scissors inwards
- drag back behind the standing leg- drag back with the sole of the foot
- drag back with the sole of the foot then exit sideways
- fake shot/double fake shot trick
- fake shot trick + dummy/jump
- stroke the ball sideways with the instep (instep/sole of the foot)
- knocking the ball quickly from right to left with the instep
- rolling the ball quickly from right to left with the sole of the foot (forward, backwards, sideways)
- stepping quickly on the ball, right/left
- 360-degree turn
- Ronaldo Trick I
- Ronaldo Trick II
- Okocha Trick
- Locomotive
- dribbling with the instep/outstep and laces
- complete turn with max. 3 touches (inside and out)
- sole of the foot forwards/backwards
- The coach can chose from this large list of skills. These exercises should be trained with a group which has already learned the skills.

Alternative: The coach sets out cones (opponents) at which the player has to complete the skills.

Note:

- High concentration in the group.
- Regularly check technique.
- The player is put under considerable pressure as he should attempt to complete the trick as quickly as possible after the call from the coach.
- Speed of anticipation, awareness and reaction are tested with the ball in this exercise. The players must also have an overview of the game and be able to see when a nearby cone is free, to avoid colliding with their teammates so that they can successfully and quickly complete the trick. It is important to remember that each trick has different characteristics.

Field size:
18-yard box

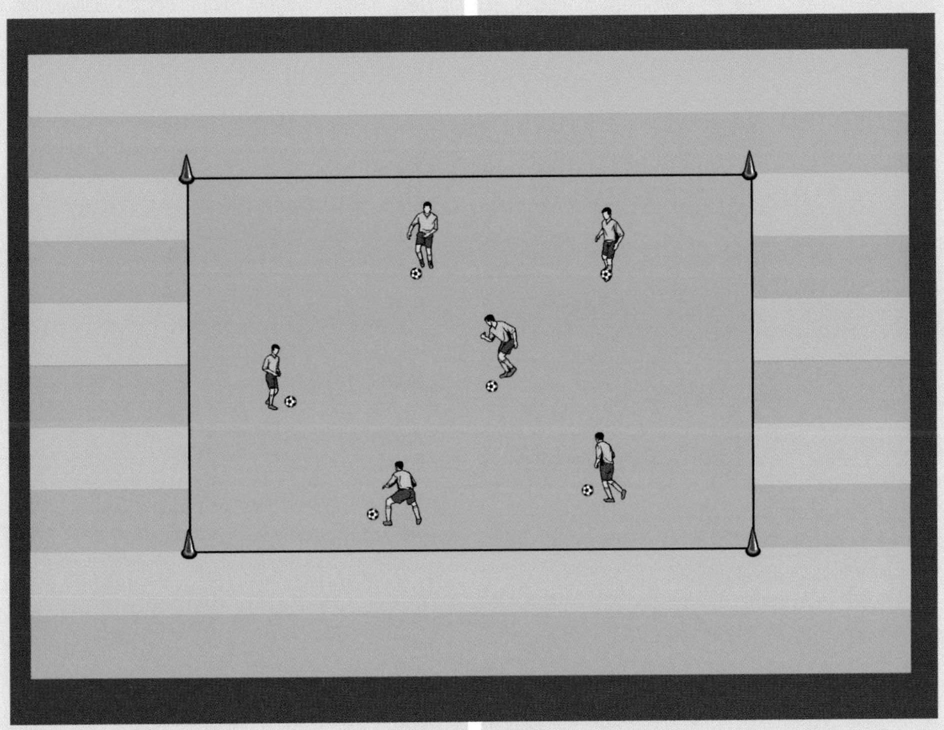

Training Target
- **Ball skill (Touch on the ball)**

Training Emphasis
- **Finesse on the ball**
- **Dribbling**

Training Aspects

Skills involved:	Outside of the foot, Controlling the ball, Inside of the foot, Variable intervals, Combining technical skill with movement, Quickness of reaction, Laces
Age level:	6-8 years, 9-12 years, 13-14 years
Level of play:	Beginner, Recreational
Type of training:	Group training
Training structure:	Warm-up, Progression, Main point/Emphasis
Purpose:	Training for fun, Attack behavior, Improve individual qualities
Total number of players:	8 or more players
Participating players:	Whole team
Training location:	Any
Spatial awareness:	Limited playing field
Duration:	10-15 min
Physiology:	Soccer-specific endurance, Explosiveness, Speed endurance, Power & Speed, Explosiveness training

Organization:
Several players (one team) start at each cone in the large box. (4 teams). If the group contains differing levels then the drills should be chosen so that the same number of circuits are completed (if necessary one player will have to go twice with a group with fewer players). One ball per team.

Implementation:
The 4 starting players start on the coach's signal at the same time and run to the next cone and back. The next player takes the ball. The players should first complete a dry run and then in a competitive situation. Run-through 2: The first player runs through the small box, to the furthest cone and back. The next player takes the ball and continues. Run-through 3: The same as 2 but that the small box (and only the small box) is a small "battleground". That means that every player in the box can attack any other player with a ball and attempt to knock his ball away. If a player loses his ball, he has to collect it and start the drill from the same position again.

Note:
- Every player goes 3 times.
- Ensure that the take is performed correctly: Right foot to right foot/left foot to left foot.
- Ensure that the take takes place at the cone.
- Attempt to have groups with similar standards.
- The cones should be encircled tightly. The ball should not be further than 50 cm from the foot.

Field size:
Large box: 15 m x 15 m
Small box: 6 m x 6 m

Distance between the cones:
Cones outer box: 15 m each.
Cones inner box: 6 m each.

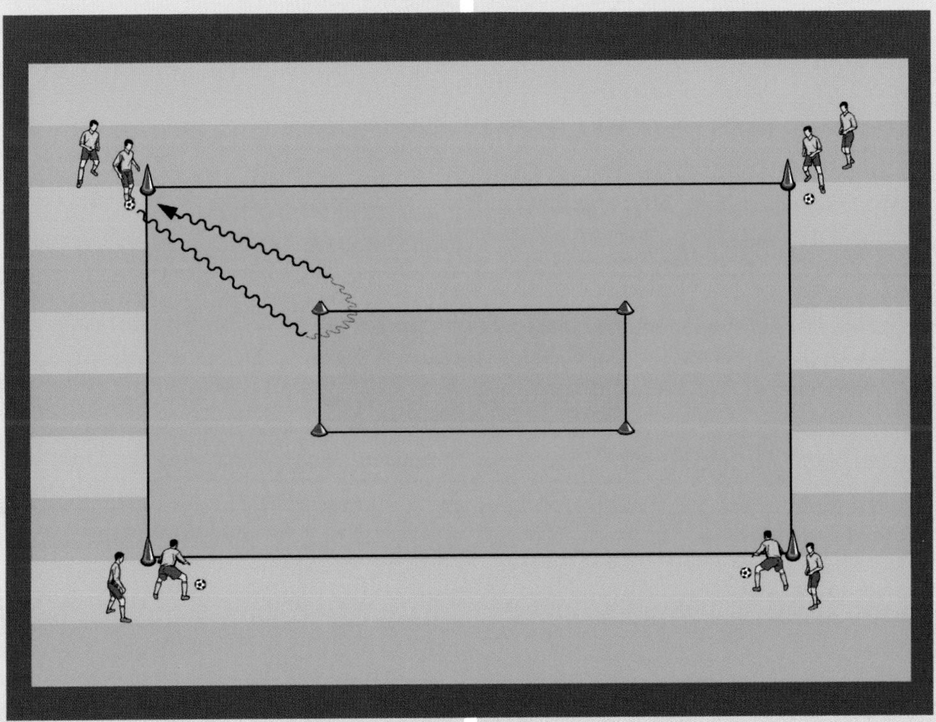

58 Shuttle Run with Tricks and Dribbling Skills

Training Target
- **Ball skill (Touch on the ball)**

Training Emphasis
- **Dribbling control**
- **Finesse on the ball**
- **Feinting/trick dribbling**
- **Fitness program**
- **Coordination**

Training Aspects

Skills involved:	**Speed of movement with ball, Quick anticipation, Outside of the foot, Trapping into space, Dribbling, Quick decision-making, Quick processing, Inside of the foot, Variable intervals, Bodyfake, Combining technical skill with movement, Speed in change of direction, Laces**
Age level:	**Any age**
Level of play:	**Recreational**
Type of training:	**Group training, Team training**
Training structure:	**Warm-up, Progression**
Purpose:	**Improve individual qualities**
Total number of players:	**12 players, 13 or more players**
Participating players:	**Whole team**
Training location:	**Indoor, Asphalt, Turf field, Grass field**
Spatial awareness:	**Limited playing field**
Duration:	**10-25 min**
Physiology:	**Soccer-specific endurance, Training of elementary endurance II, Explosiveness, Speed endurance, Power & Speed**

Organization:
Set up 9 stations with cones within the box. 2 players start at 6 of the outer cones. One ball per player.

Implementation:
The players start one after another from each of the bottom cones:
1. The players A, B and C dribble at the same time with the ball around the middle cone and then pass to the opposing player and follow their pass with a sprint. The player receiving the ball dribbles straight back into the box and completes the drill from the other side.
2. Same sequence, however the cone is dribbled around using the outside of the foot.
3. Perform trick in front of the cone before the opposing player takes the ball. Make sure that the ball is taken with the same foot as used by the player previously in possession. Practice all tricks!
4. All exercises can also include a competitive edge. The loser has to do press-ups!

Note:
- High concentration.
- Tidy technical completion.
- Correct timing when controlling the ball (the signal is the movement of the player in possession).
- The distance between the players should be as small as possible.

- The tricks should be carried out at the same time (approx. 2 meters in front of the middle cone).
- Precise passing, demand strong passes played to the correct foot.
- Communication.

Field size:
20 x 20 m

Distance between the cones:
10 m

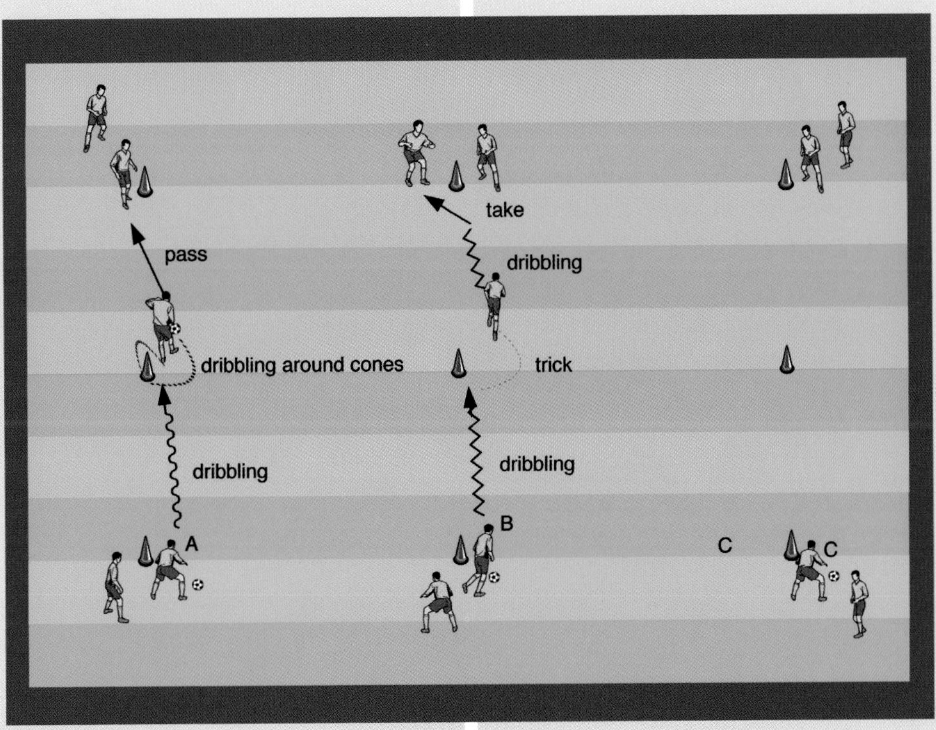

59 Technique Exercise: Box/Cube-Five

Training Target
- **Ball skill (Touch on the ball)**

Training Emphasis
- **Dribbling control**
- **Finesse on the ball**
- **Feinting/trick dribbling**
- **Fitness program**
- **Coordination**

Training Aspects

Skills involved:	Speed of movement with ball, Quick anticipation, Outside of the foot
Age level:	9-12 years, 13-14 years, 15-16 years
Level of play:	Recreational
Type of training:	Group training
Training structure:	Warm-up, Main point/Emphasis
Purpose:	Improve individual qualities
Total number of players:	4 or more players
Participating players:	Whole team
Training location:	Indoor, Asphalt, Turf field, Grass field
Spatial awareness:	Limited playing field
Duration:	20-40 min
Physiology:	Soccer-specific endurance, Training of elementary endurance II, Speed endurance, Power & Speed

Organization:
Set up a box with cones. 4 players start at each cone, place a cone/pole/flag in the middle.

Implementation:
The first players at cones A and D start dribbling towards the center marking and carry out a trick (called from the coach) just before the marker. After the marker, the players dribble diagonally to the opposite cone. The first players at cones B and C then start with the same procedure as soon as players A and D have passed the middle marker.

Variation:
The players dribble towards the marker in the middle, complete the trick called out by the coach and then dribble back to their original cone.

Note:
- It is essential that the players start at the same time.
- If the players have to complete a dummy-shot trick then they must complete them at the same time and ensure that they both complete the trick with the same foot and pass the middle marker on opposite sides.
- Fundamentally the following rules should be followed when completing all tricks: tricks are feints. As a result the position of the upper body is important. It is the movement of the upper body which distracts the opponent. Drills should always be trained with both feet. Players should have as many touches on the ball as possible, always have the ball under control, control the ball close to their body so that their opponent cannot get to the ball. The trick should be carried out approx. 1-2 meters from the cone, which represents an opponent.

Field size:
24 x 24 m

Distance between the cones:
12 m wide; 12 m long.
The middle cone/pole/flag is centrally placed in the box.

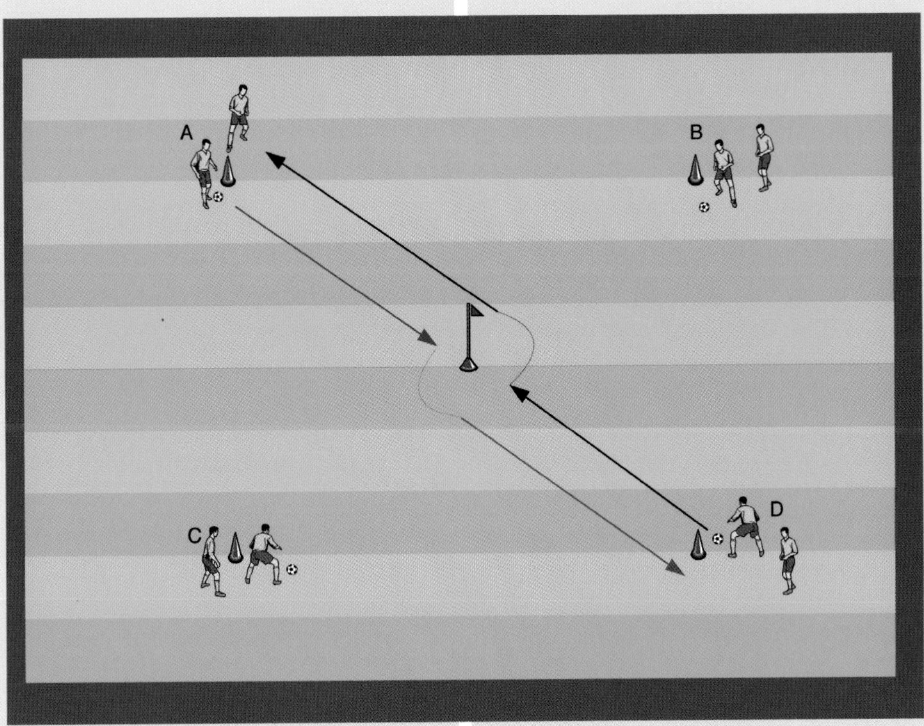

60 Skills Exercise: Christmas Tree

Training Target

- Ball skill (Touch on the ball)

Training Emphasis

- Dribbling control
- Finesse on the ball
- Feinting/trick dribbling
- Fitness program
- Coordination

Training Aspects

Skills involved:	Speed of movement with ball, Quick anticipation, Outside of the foot, Control, Trapping into space, Dribbling, Quick decision-making, Quick processing, Inside of the foot, Bodyfake, Combining technical skill with movement, Quickness of reaction, Speed in change of direction, Laces
Age level:	Any age
Level of play:	Recreational
Type of training:	Team training
Training structure:	Warm-up, Progression, Main point/Emphasis
Purpose:	Attack behavior, Improve individual qualities
Total number of players:	4 or more players
Participating players:	Whole team
Training location:	Any
Spatial awareness:	Limited playing field
Duration:	10-30 min
Physiology:	Soccer-specific endurance, Training of elementary endurance II, Training of elementary endurance I, Strength endurance, Speed endurance, Power & Speed

Organization:
Set up an obstacle course. The yellow cones are always placed in the middle of the red cones.

Implementation:
The players start from the four starting points and move right to the yellow cone, then left to the red cone with the ball at their feet. The players should turn in front of the cones, not behind the cones.

Exercise 1: clip the ball with the instep in front of each cone.
Exercise 2: clip the ball with the outstep in front of each cone.
Exercise 3: step over in front of each cone.
Exercise 4: turn 360 degrees in front of each cone.
Exercise 5: fake shot trick in front of each cone.
Exercise 6: complete each of the five previous skills one after another, so that everything that has previously been learned can be practiced in one go.

Note:
The exercise should be started slowly with the focus on the quality of the tricks. Technical quality is more important than speed. As the player becomes more confident, the speed and complexity of the drill can be increased. The following players should not start too soon and need to

ensure that they reduce their speed if a player in front of them makes a mistake and so slows the drill.

Field size:
36 m long and 24 m wide.

Distance between the cones:
The distances between the red cones is 12 m and the yellow cones are 6 m away from the red cones.

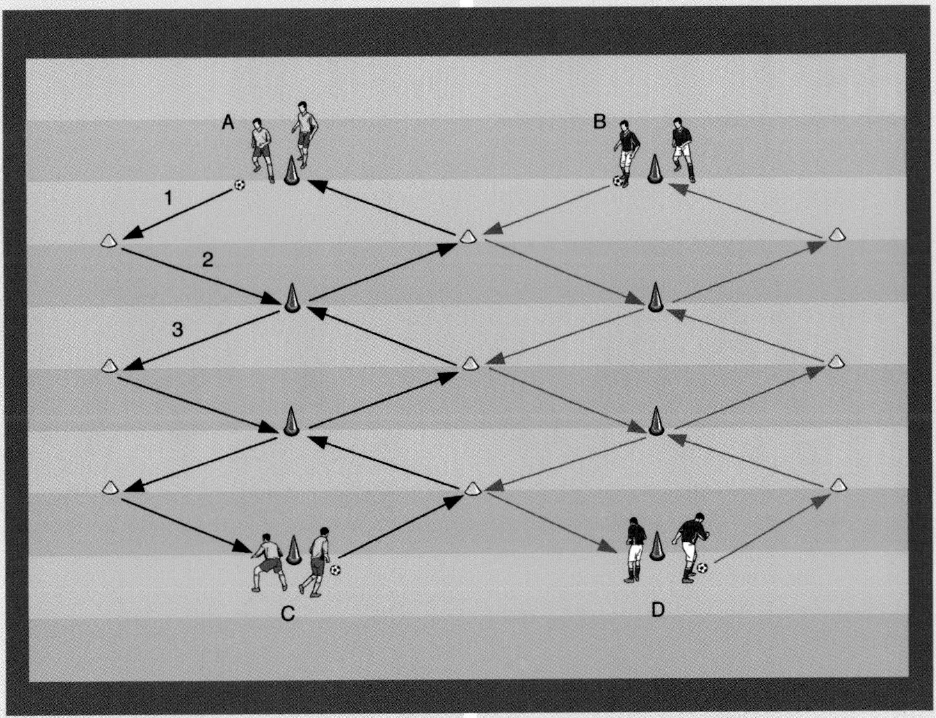

Training Target
- **Ball skill (Touch on the ball)**

Training Emphasis
- **Dribbling control**
- **Finesse on the ball**

Training Aspects

Skills involved:	Speed of movement with ball, Controlling the ball, Combining technical skill with movement, Short passing
Age level:	Any age
Level of play:	Recreational
Type of training:	Group training, Mid-size group training 5-8 players
Training structure:	Progression
Purpose:	Attack behavior, Improve individual qualities
Total number of players:	6 or more players
Participating players:	Whole team
Training location:	Any
Spatial awareness:	Limited playing field
Duration:	10-15 min
Physiology:	Soccer-specific endurance, Speed endurance, Power & Speed

Organization:
Two group start at opposite cones. One ball per group.

Implementation:
The first player of each group has a ball. Both players start dribbling towards the other side at the same time. The player waiting for the ball moves towards the player in possession 1-2 meters and takes the ball whilst moving forwards.

Note:
- Call for top speed.
- Close dribbling.
- Both players must keep an eye on one another to avoid collision.
- The ball should be dribbled with the laces/outside of the foot and not with the instep.
- To be able to use the right dribbling technique, the players' ankles should be opened with their toes pointing downwards.
- The two players waiting for the ball should start without a ball just before the player in possession reaches the cone. This will ensure that the ball is taken on the move. Ball control and "takes" are practiced as a result and this also ensures that the players keep the tempo high.
- If the player takes the ball on the move with the instep, then the movement of the foot should flow downwards. The upper body should be lightly leaning over the ball. When the ball is controlled with the outside of the foot, the upper body should be slightly turned inwards. The foot should (also) be lightly turned inwards. The ankle should be open.

Field size:
6 x 20 m

Distance between the cones:
approx. 20 m

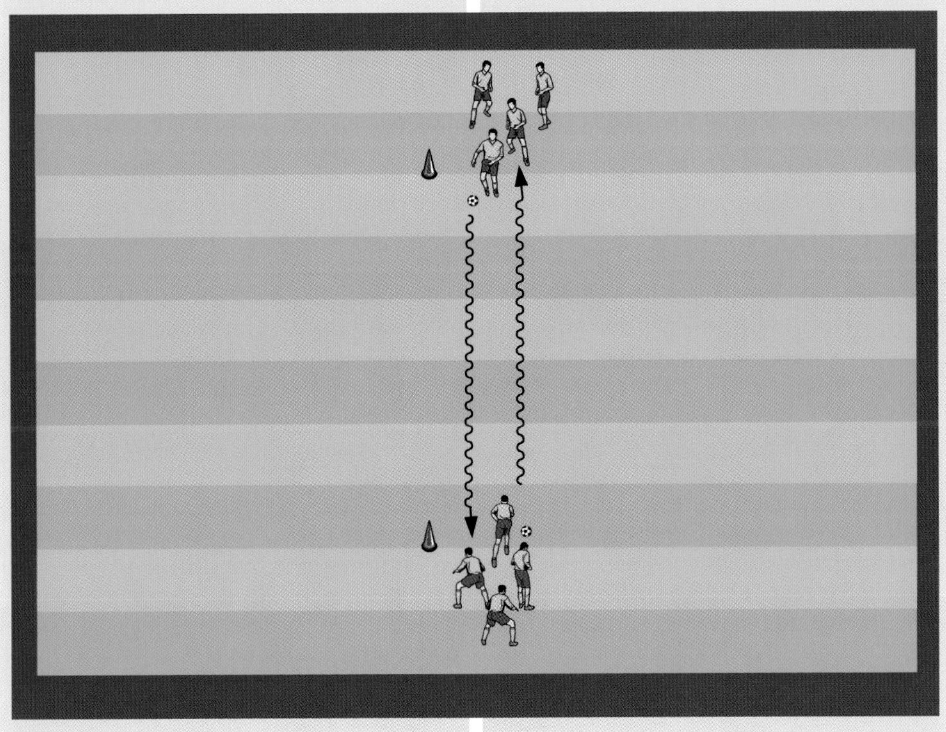

Training Target
- **Ball skill (Touch on the ball)**

Training Emphasis
- **Dribbling control**
- **Finesse on the ball**
- **Fitness program**

Training Aspects

Skills involved:	**Speed of movement with ball, Quick anticipation, Outside of the foot, Controlling the ball, Control, Dribbling, Inside of the foot, Inside of the foot passing, Laces, Quick understanding of danger**
Age level:	**9-12 years, 13-14 years, 15 years to Adult**
Level of play:	**Advanced**
Type of training:	**Small group training 2-6 players, Team training**
Training structure:	**Warm-up, Progression**
Purpose:	**Improve individual qualities**
Total number of players:	**4 or more players**
Participating players:	**Whole team**
Training location:	**Any**
Spatial awareness:	**Limited playing field**
Duration:	**10-20 min**
Physiology:	**Soccer-specific endurance, Speed endurance, Power & Speed**

Organization:
Two players positioned at 2 cones placed opposite each other. Three balls at each cone.

Implementation:
The focus of this exercise is dribbling techniques, combined with takes at high speed. After each action, the player should complete a short sprint. One player starts with a ball and passes in space to the middle of the exercise area to the player opposite who moves towards the ball. This player attempts to control the ball with his first touch and to then dribble to the other cone. The other player then 'takes' the ball in the middle of the exercise area. If the player in possession dribbles with his right foot, then the ball should also be taken by the other player with his right foot. The players can decide which foot they would like to complete the exercise. The 'take' should take place when the players are approx. 1 m apart. It is not a pass. Due to the tight space the player receiving the ball will not be able to control the pass effectively. Subsequently, the first two players pass to their opposite partners who have moved towards the ball. The pass would occur when the players are approx. 2-3 m apart.

Alternative:
- Each player dribbles at speed to the opposite cone.
- The players dribble identical paths with two balls.
- The players have three balls.

Note:
- The player without a ball starts when the player in possession starts (start timing).

- Correct start position. (If the player dribbles with his left foot then the opposing player must position himself to be able to take the ball with his left foot.)
- The take shouldn't happen too far apart.
- The pass shouldn't be played too late.
- The pass must be played into space in front of the player receiving the ball and not be hit straight at the player.
- The strength of the pass and the precision of the pass are important and should be demanded by the coach.
- If the player passes with his right foot, then the pass should arrive at the opposing player's right foot.
- The timing of the pass must be correct (i.e. not too late).
- During the exercise the players must communicate with one another.
- Short, quick movements when dribbling.
- The ball should not be more than 50cm from the players' feet.
- Both feet should be used when dribbling. All dribbling techniques should be used (instep, outstep, laces).

Field size:
Two cones 15 m apart.

Distance between the cones:
15 m

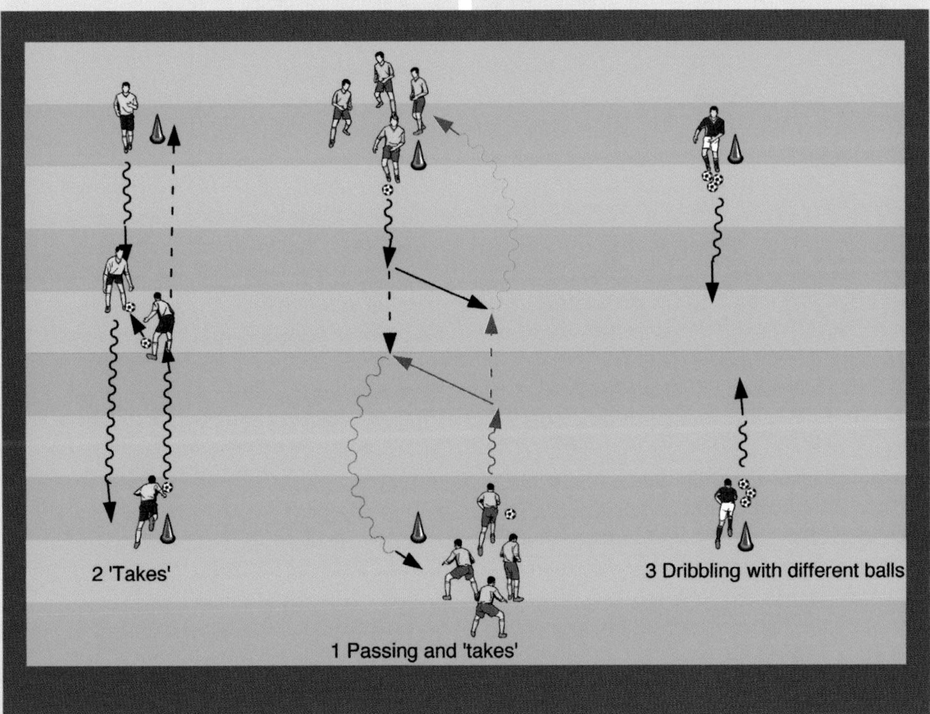

Training Target
- Ball skill (Touch on the ball)

Training Emphasis
- Dribbling control
- Finesse on the ball
- Feinting/trick dribbling
- Fitness program

Training Aspects

Skills involved:	Speed of movement with ball, Quick anticipation, Controlling the ball, Dribbling Quick decision-making, Quick processing, Combining technical skill with movement, Short passing
Age level:	9-12 years, 13-14 years, 15-16 years
Level of play:	Recreational
Type of training:	Individual training, Group training
Training structure:	Warm-up, Progression, Main point/Emphasis
Purpose:	Improve individual qualities
Total number of players:	2 or more players
Participating players:	Whole team
Training location:	Any
Spatial awareness:	Limited playing field
Duration:	10-20 min
Physiology:	Soccer-specific endurance, Power & Speed

Organization:
Two groups begin opposite each other at two cones. The cones are approx. 25 meters apart. One ball per group.

Implementation:
The first players of each group dribble at the same time towards each other. When they are approx. 3-4 meters apart they carry out a trick to out-maneuver their opponent and pass (or give the ball) to the opposite group. This sequence repeats itself over and again with different tricks and feints. Possible tricks are: a.) step-over b.) pirouette c.) shot dummy d.) In- and outstep e.) backheel* f.) stroking the ball with the sole of the foot/instep g.) dragging the ball back h.) laces + outstep i.) Okocha Trick* If the coach calls backheel (the players should abruptly change direction and head off in the other direction), the ball is then not passed to the opposing group but given back to the starting group.

Note:
- The two active players must start at the same time.
- The tricks must be timed correctly (not too early and not too late). The correct distance to carry out the trick is approx. 3-4 meters for this exercise (because both players approach each other at speed. If the player with the ball approaches a waiting player the distance should be reduced to 2m).
- The tricks must be carried out by both players with the same foot, otherwise the players would collide. This means that the players have to quickly agree which side to dribble with before each exercise begins.
- The trick must be correctly carried out and at top speed. After the opponent has been passed, each player should make a short sprint of about 2-3 meters.
- The subsequent pass should be played hard along the floor.

- The player waiting for the pass should move towards the pass after having made a short dummy run away from the ball and should control the ball with his first touch.
- Pay attention that the players start at the cones otherwise the distance between the players will become irregular.
- It is important that the player uses his upper body to distract his opponent from the trick as opponents usually focus on players' upper bodies.
- The pass must be hit in space for the opposing player to run on to.

Field size:
6 x 25 m

Distance between the cones:
Approx. 25 m

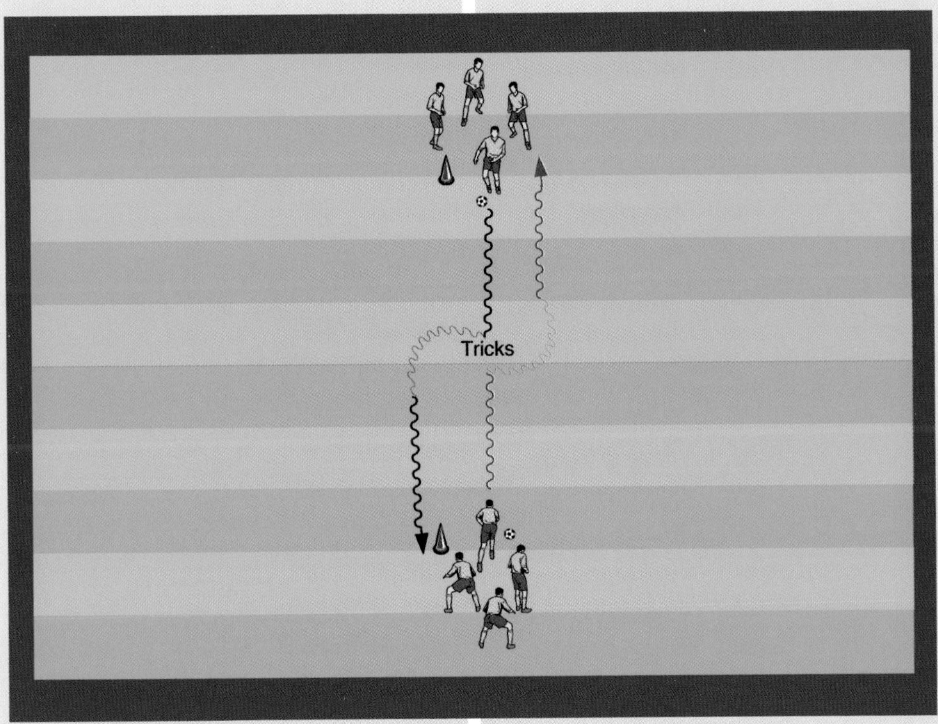

Training Target
- **Ball skill (Touch on the ball)**

Training Emphasis
- **Dribbling control**
- **Finesse on the ball**
- **Feinting/trick dribbling**
- **Fitness program**

Training Aspects

Skills involved:	**Speed of movement with ball, Quick anticipation, Dribbling, Quick decision-making, Inside of the foot passing, Inside of the laces passing,, Bodyfake, Combining technical skill with movement**
Age level:	**6-8 years, 9-12 years, 13-14 years**
Level of play:	**Recreational**
Type of training:	**Group training**
Training structure:	**Main point/Emphasis**
Purpose:	**Attack behavior**
Total number of players:	**2 or more players**
Participating players:	**Whole team**
Training location:	**Any**
Spatial awareness:	**Limited playing field**
Duration:	**10-15 min**
Physiology:	**Soccer-specific endurance, Speed endurance, Power & Speed**

Organization:
Set up the cones with a mini goal as shown. The group starts at the first cone. One ball per player. If this is not possible then each player should be instructed to collect their ball after they have shot and pass it to the next waiting player.

Implementation:
Each player begins at the first cone by dribbling at speed towards the first cone and then dribbles around the cone on the left side, to then be able to flick the ball to the right. He approaches the cone from the right, dribbles around it and then dribbles at top speed to the next cone. At that cone, the player turns towards the goal and then dribbles in tempo for the next 2m towards the next cone. He dummies this cone and then dribbles to the last cone. The player should then finish with his right foot. The player should then make a short sprint towards the last cone to finish with his left foot. The players should alternately approach the cones so that they shoot first with their left foot and then with their right foot for each drill. The player then joins the back of the group.

Note:
- Close control (the ball shouldn't be further than 50cm from the foot).
- Top speed.
- The ball should always be dribbled around the cone with the foot furthest away from the cone.
- The change of direction should be completed immediately behind the cone. This trick then resembles actual game play.
- The coach can also stand in place of the "trick cone." This increases the resemblance to actual game play.
- The shot at goal should occur immediately after the player has passed the final cone.

Field size:
14 x 34 m

Distance between the cones:
Start cone - cone 1: 7 m cone 1 - cone 2: 7 m cone 2 - cone 3: 7 m cone 1 - cone 3: 5 m cone 3 - cone 4 (trick cone): 7 m cone 4 - cone 5: 5 m cone 5 - goal: 10 m

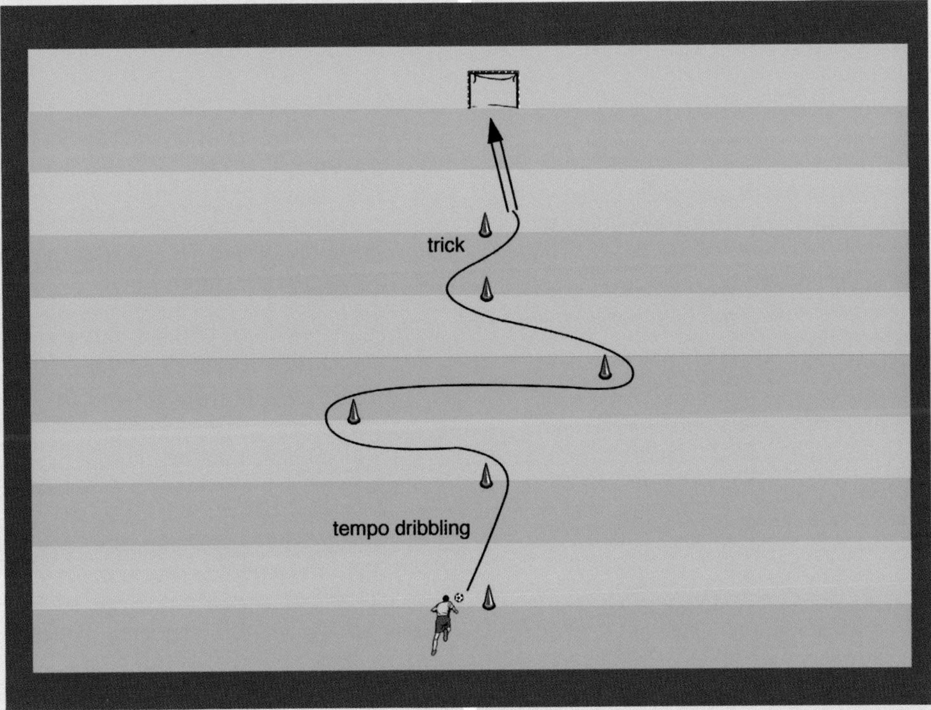

Training Target

- **Ball skill (Touch on the ball)**

Training Emphasis

- **Dribbling control**
- **Finesse on the ball**
- **Feinting/trick dribbling**
- **Fitness program**

Training Aspects

Skills involved:	Speed of movement with ball, Control Dribbling, Quick decision-making, Inside of the foot passing, Inside of the laces passing, Bodyfake, Combining technical skill with movement, Laces
Age level:	6-8 years, 9-12 years, 13-14 years
Level of play:	Recreational
Type of training:	Team training
Training structure:	Progression, Main point/Emphasis
Purpose:	Attack behavior, Improve individual qualities
Total number of players:	4 or more players
Participating players:	Whole team
Training location:	any
Spatial awareness:	Limited playing field
Duration:	10-15 min
Physiology:	Soccer-specific endurance, Speed endurance, Power & Speed

Organization:
Set up the cones with a mini goal as shown. The group starts at the first cone. One ball per player. If this is not possible then each player should be instructed to collect their ball after they have shot and pass it to the next waiting player.

Implementation:
Each player begins at the first cone by dribbling at speed towards the first cone and then dribbles around the cone on the right side to then be able to flick the ball to the left. He approaches the cone from the left, dribbles around it and then dribbles at top speed to the next cone. At that cone, the player turns towards the goal and then dribbles in tempo for the next 2m towards the second to last cone before the goal. He dummies this cone and then dribbles to the left to the last cone. The player should then finish with his left foot. The player should then make a short sprint towards the last cone to finish with his left foot. The players should alternately approach the cones so that they shoot first with their right foot and then with their left foot. The player then joins the back of the group.

Note:

- Close control (the ball shouldn't be further than 50 cm from the foot).
- Top speed.
- The ball should always be dribbled around the cone with the foot furthest away from the cone.
- The change of direction should be completed immediately behind the cone. This trick then resembles actual game play.

- The coach can also stand in place of the "trick cone." This increases the resemblance to actual game play.
- The shot at goal should occur immediately after the player has passed the final cone.

Field size:
14 x 34 m

Distance between the cones:
Start cone - cone 1: 7 m cone 1 - cone 3: 7 m cone 1 - cone 4: 12 m cone 1 - cone 2: 7 m cone 2 - cone 3: 14 m cone 3 - cone 4 (trick cone): 7 m cone 4 - cone 5: 5 m cone 5 - to goal: 10 m

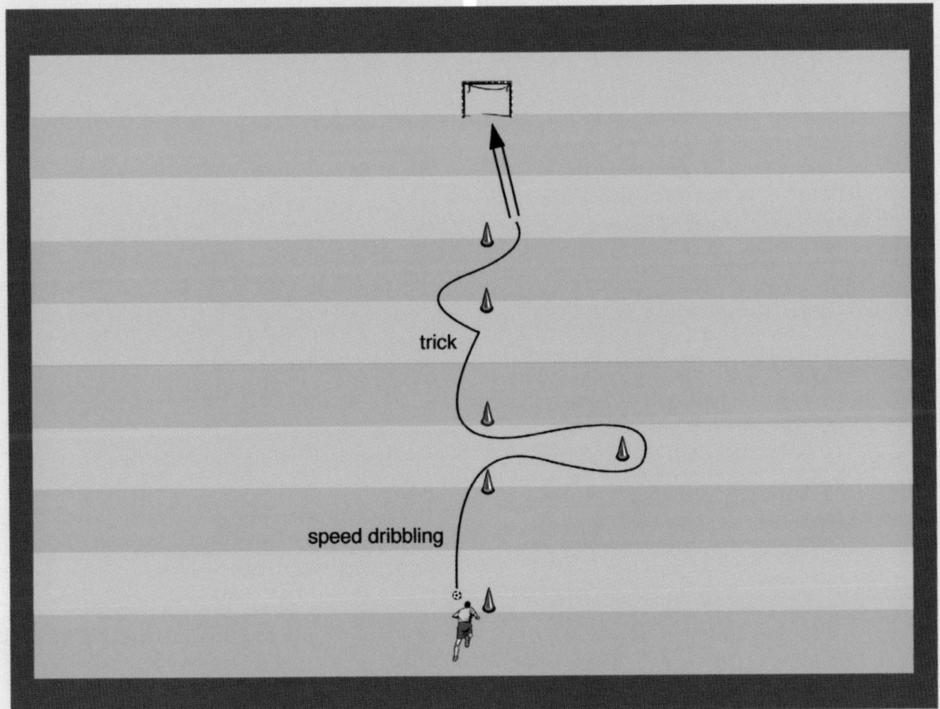

Training Target

- **Ball skill (Touch on the ball)**

Training Emphasis

- **Dribbling control**
- **Finesse on the ball**
- **Feinting/trick dribbling**
- **Fitness program**

Training Aspects

Skills involved:	Speed of movement with ball, Offensive play, Quick anticipation, Outside of the foot, Dribbling, Quick decision-making, Quick processing, Inside of the foot, Combining technical skill with movement, Short passing, Quickness of reaction,, Jump technique (parcour), Quick understanding of danger
Age level:	6-8 years, 9 -12 years, 13- 14 years, 15-16 years
Level of play:	Recreational
Type of training:	Group training
Training structure:	Warm-up, Progression, Main point/Emphasis
Purpose:	Improve individual qualities
Total number of players:	12 players, 13 or more players
Participating players:	Whole team
Training location:	Any
Spatial awareness:	Limited playing field
Duration:	10-15 min
Physiology:	Soccer-specific endurance, Power & Speed

Organization:
Two groups of 5 stand opposite each other in lines at either side of the box. The players should be approx. 5 meters apart. Both front players (see graphic) should start with a ball and start facing the other players. A ball should be played at each diagonally opposite cone.

Implementation:
The starting player runs slalom through the other players in his group. He dribbles through the players and uses the same (or different) trick before each player before dribbling past him. The "obstacle players" should jog slowly towards the player with the ball. The player closest to the starting cone then collects a ball from the starting cone and begins to dribble through the "obstacle players." When each player has completed the slalom dribble, he passes to the player at the start of the other group and joins the back of this group. The players change groups at the end of each drill.

Note:
- This exercise only works when both teams dribble at the same speed. To achieve this, they must observe one another and communicate to the player with the ball how fast he should dribble.
- The distance between the players must remain the same, so that the player with the ball has the opportunity to correctly carry out his trick.
- The player with the ball is forced to regularly look up by the movement of the players towards him.
- The players approaching the player with the ball should not approach too fast otherwise the distances between players will become irregular.

- Close & tight control is essential to completing this exercise successfully.
- The dribbler must keep his eye on both the ball and the opponent.
- The last pass must be hit precisely to the other side and communicated by way of a short call.

Distance between the cones:
width 10 m, length 30 m.

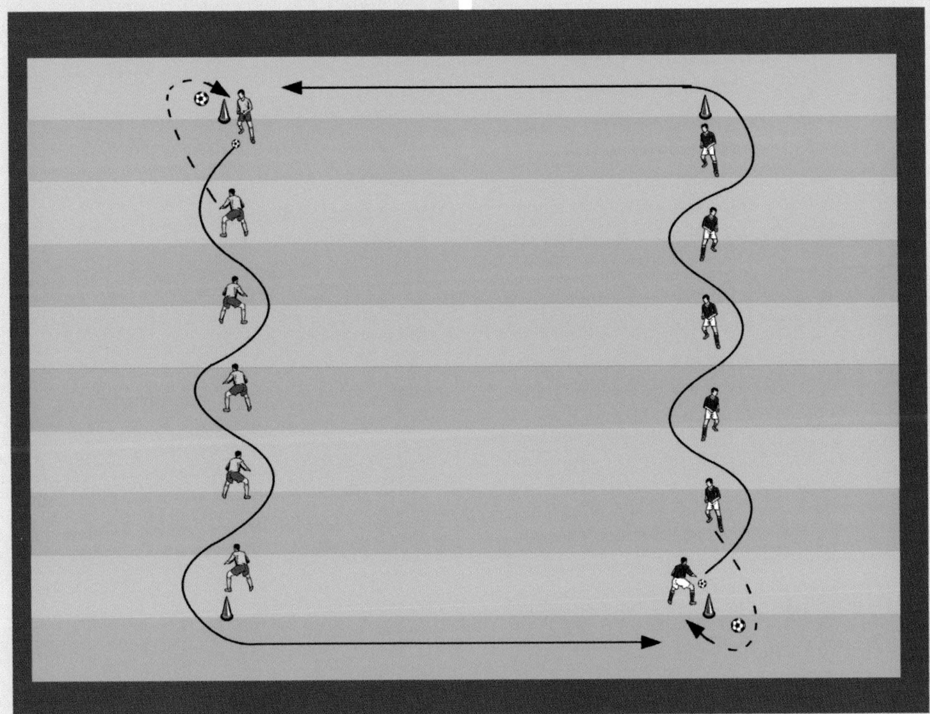

67 Touch - Football Tennis

Training Target
- **Ball skill (Touch on the ball)**

Training Emphasis
- **Trapping**
- **Finesse on the ball**
- **Lifting the ball**
- **Ball control**
- **Fun games**
- **Juggling techniques**

Training Aspects

Skills involved:	Speed of movement with ball, Quick anticipation, Trapping, Controlling the ball, Control, One touch passes, Half-volley, Quick decision-making, Bicycle kicks, Quick processing, Inside of the foot, Inside of the foot passing, Inside of the laces passing, Combinations, Combining technical skill with movement, Heading from a jump, Heading from a standstill, Heading while in motion, Passing in a triangle, Quickness of reaction, Volley, Laces, Quick understanding of danger
Age level:	13-14 years, 15-16 years, 15 years to Adult
Level of play:	Recreational
Type of training:	Group training
Training structure:	Main point/Emphasis
Purpose:	Training for fun, Motivational training, Improve individual qualities
Total number of players:	2 or more players
Participating players:	Whole team
Training location:	Indoor, Asphalt, Turf field, Grass field
Spatial awareness:	Limited playing field
Duration:	60-70 min
Physiology:	Soccer-specific endurance

Organization:
Set up a head-tennis court 8 x 16 meters. The net in the middle should have a height of 1.5 meters. A 3-meter-wide corridor made up of cones can also be used instead of the net.

Implementation:
The service should come as a volley or a drop-kick. The ball can bounce once and each team is allowed max. three touches (the ball must be returned over the net with the third touch). A new player must touch the ball after each touch. Every rally won/lost is rewarded with a point. The team which won the last point serves. A new player serves every time his team has the serve. Each set is played to 21 (by two clear points), i.e. if the score is 21:20 then at least one more point must be played, etc. The coach can decide how many sets are played. Normally 2 or 3.

Note:
- The teams can be made up of 1-4 players. 2 v 2 or 3 v 3 is ideal so that each player has enough touches on the ball.

- 1 v 1 can be very intensive. The players train their close control, coordination and ball skills intensively.
- The coach can vary the amount of touches allowed by each player.
- **Tip:** If possible the players should try to control the ball with their first touch and then let it bounce before hitting the ball calmly back over the next with their next touch.
- The players are, of course, allowed to control the ball with all parts of the body (except with their hand). The ball shouldn't only be headed back and forth. The focus is on footwork and ball skills.

Field size:
Court size 10-16 m long and between 6-8 m wide. The size of the court depends upon the number of player taking part.

Distance between the cones:
width: 6-8 m
length (per court): 10-16 m, in total 20-32 m

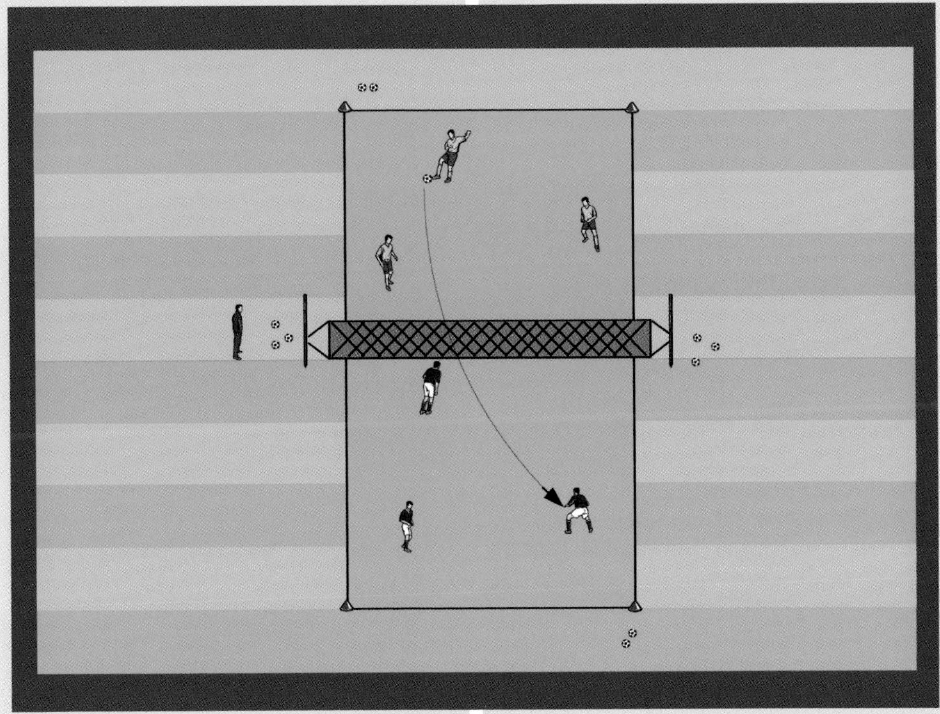

Training Target

- Ball skill (Touch on the ball)

Training Emphasis

- Trapping
- Finesse on the ball
- Lifting the ball
- Ball control
- Fun games
- Juggling techniques
- Position play

Training Aspects

Skills involved:	Speed of movement with ball, Quick anticipation, Control, One touch passes, Half-volley, Quick decision-making, Bicycle kicks, Quick processing, Inside of the foot, Inside of the foot passing, Inside of the laces passing, Combining technical skill with movement, Heading from a jump, Heading from a standstill, Heading while in motion, Quickness of reaction, Volley, Laces, Quick understanding of danger
Age level:	13 - 14 years, 15 - 16 years, 15 years to Adult, 17 years to Adult
Level of play:	Recreational
Type of training:	Group training
Training structure:	Conclusion, Progression, Main point/Emphasis
Purpose:	Training for fun, Improve individual qualities
Total number of players:	4 or more players
Participating players:	Whole team
Training location:	Indoor, Asphalt, Turf field, Grass field
Spatial awareness:	Limited playing field
Duration:	10-30 min
Physiology:	Soccer-specific endurance

Organization:
Set up a head-tennis court 8 x 16 meters. The net in the middle should have a height of 1.5 meters. A 3-meter-wide corridor made up of cones can also be used instead of the net.

Implementation:
The service should come as a volley or a drop-kick. The player must try to run around to the other side of the net and join onto the back of the waiting team after he has knocked the ball over the net. The ball can bounce once and each player is allowed max. two touches. After returning the ball the player then runs to the other side of the net. If a player hits the ball into the net, hits the ball out or is not able to return the ball with his second touch then he is out.
The final is played "best of 5" between the last two remaining players. Each mistake (net/out/extra touch) results in a point for the opponent.

Note:

- The coach can vary the amount of touches allowed by each player.
- Tip: If possible the players should try to control the ball with their first touch and then let it bounce before hitting the ball calmly back over the next with their next touch.

- The players are, of course, allowed to control the ball with all parts of the body (except with their hand). The ball shouldn't only be headed back and forth. The focus is on footwork and ball skills.

Field size:
length 16 m width 8 m

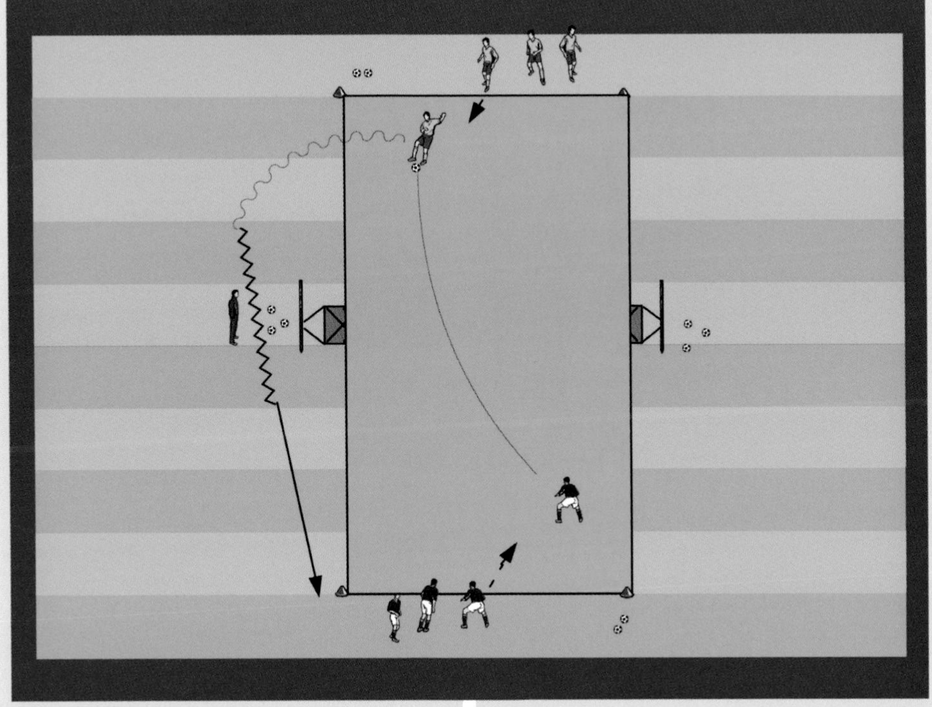

D. Brueggemann
Soccer Alive –
The Game is the Best Teacher

ISBN: 9781841262352
$ 19.95 US / $ 32.95 AUS
£ 12.95 UK / € 19.95

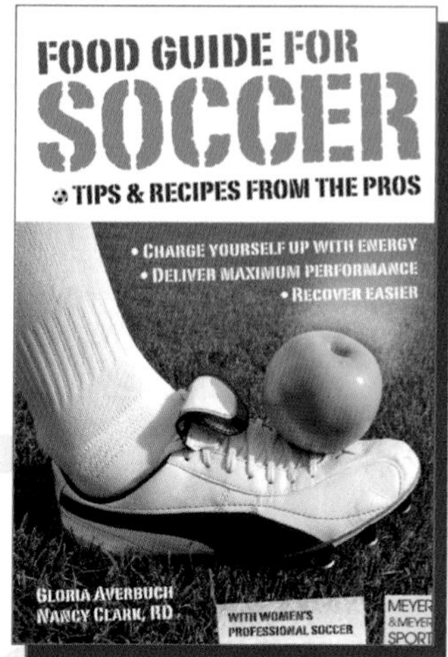

Gloria Averbuch & Nancy Clark, RD
Food Guide for Soccer -
Tips & Recipes from the Pros

ISBN 9781841262888
$ 18.95 US / $ 32.95 AUS
£ 14.95 UK / € 18.95

Gerhard Frank
Soccer Training Programs

ISBN: 9781841262741
$ 17.95 US / $ 29.95 AUS
£ 12.95 UK / € 16.95

Dooley Soccer University
Thomas Dooley & Christian Titz
Passing & Ball Control

ISBN: 9781841263007
$ 16.95 US/$ 29.95 AUS
£ 12.95 UK / € 16.95

Ralf Meier
Strength Training for Soccer

ISBN: 9781841262086
$ 16.95 US / $ 29.95 AUS
£ 12.95 UK / € 16.95

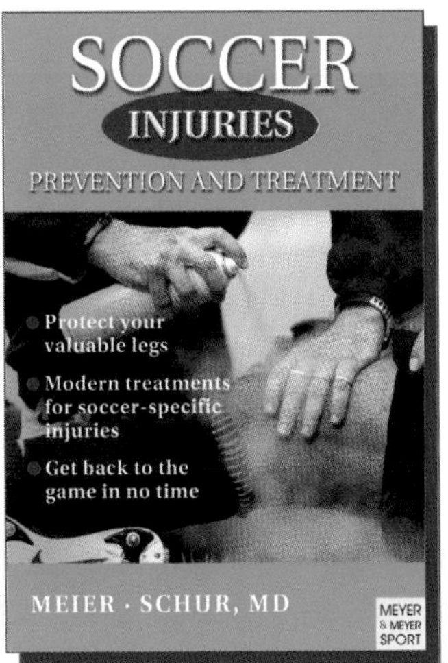

Ralf Meier/Andreas Schur, MD
Soccer Injuries

ISBN: 9781841262376
$ 16.95 US / $ 29.95 AUS
£ 12.95 UK / € 16.95

Peter Schreiner
Soccer – Perfect Ball Control

ISBN: 9781841262789
$ 16.95 US / $ 29.95 AUS
£ 12.95 UK / € 16.95

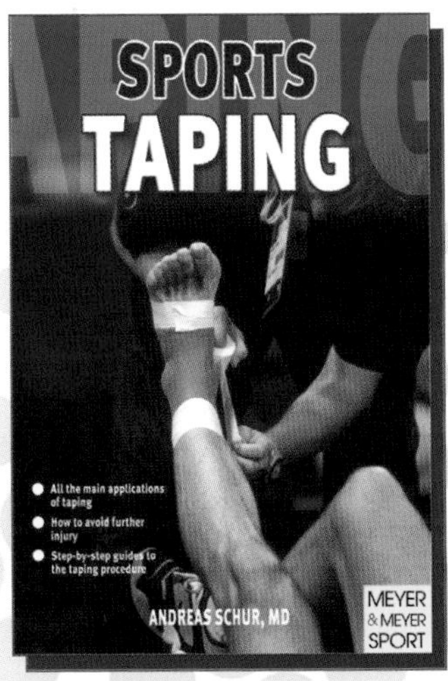

Andreas Schur, MD
Sports Taping

ISBN: 9781841262093
$ 16.95 US / $ 29.95 AUS
£ 12.95 UK / € 16.95